Copyright © 2006 Celeste A. Frazier
All rights reserved.
ISBN: 1-4196-2704-X

To order additional copies, please contact us.
BookSurge, LLC
www.booksurge.com
1-866-308-6235
orders@booksurge.com

In Spirit, In Love

Celeste A. Frazier

2006

ACKNOWLEDGMENTS

I thank my mother for her unconditional love. I thank my minister, Reverend Michael Bernard Beckwith, who helped me to discover Who I Am in Truth. Thanks to Cora Moncrief for proofing my first draft and convincing me to preface the book. I am grateful for her uninformed read of a carefree mystic. I am grateful for all of the people who encouraged me to write and publish my writings. I am grateful for Sunshine Daye's generosity in licensing her photographs to me for this book. I thank my Muse, my Lover, my Authentic Self, God, for creating this work through me.

This book is dedicated to my father, Freddie Frazier Jr. for he is a role model of strength, perseverence and tenacity.

PREFACE

This book is an exposé of my trysts with Spirit. In the course of my numinous moments, I have, on occasion, been able to document some of what has come through my mind and my heart in this book. I have summoned Spirit more frequently than before and because of this, I feel a growing intimacy into the unknown frontiers that seemed inaccessible in the past. I am grateful that the doors and windows of my psyche are opening up to receive all that I can.

My initial intention was simply to write a book of inspirational poetry. However, my journey into spiritual practices, counseling and study have led me down many avenues of thought and exploration of the spiritual nature of the universe. Some of the contents of this book have come from my studies or talks that I have given. As I uncover many mysteries of the known/unknown workings of Life in the absolute, I continue to reveal to myself how little I know. I merely offer this perspective as an option or a stepping stone on your journey.

Although a couple of pieces were written prior to my commitment to membership at the Agape International Center of Truth, the majority of these writings come from my walk through Religious Science. Religious Science, also known as the Science of Mind, was founded by Ernest Holmes in the early part of the Twentieth Century. It came through the realm of New Thought which was a new way of thinking about God as an internal Power/Presence that we can use to co-create our lives.

Many of my teachers referenced in my essays are people I have not personally met but who have shed light on matters of spirituality through their writings or speeches. They are mentioned here out of deference to the light that shines within each of them. Each one has contributed to my healing and growth. And yet there remain so many, who are unnamed, who have also been my teachers. I honor the Light in us all.

ALL

It's powerful, strong and rigid

and yet it is fluid and calm.

It is simply All.

ARE YOU CONVINCED?

Do you believe? Ernest Holmes, the founder of Religious Science, suggests to us that "God comes silent and alone to each one of us in the stillness of our own souls." He further suggests that we "...take time daily to sense God's Presence in us, to believe in it, and to accept Its completeness in our life."

What does it mean to believe in God? Every day, we have an opportunity to look at our lives and see what we believe about God. There is so much on the airwaves about God. There is much on the Internet about God. There is much in history about the actions taken with a belief in God. As a Religious Scientist, I don't doubt that people believe in God. Even atheists have a belief in what God is supposed to be, I would think. And I presume that the claim of being an atheist is a claim of denying the God that others want them to believe in. Atheists may not have evidence of the existence of such a God.

It's these kind of thoughts that make me question what kind of God we believe in. And I say "we" because what you think is part of the subjective that I am living in. What you believe is going to be something that I encounter in some way. And it may effect my belief on some level because each belief is an idea, a thought – with which I, on occasion, must contend.

We hear the expression, God is in control of the Universe. We look at the Universe and see genocide, war and other crimes and we want to blame God. In a class I once facilitated, a student did not understand why we Religious Scientists think that there is no evil. He mentioned Hitler, 9/11, and other things to question that idea. He mentioned the tsunami and how that was good because people were helping one another. I asked him what he saw on 9/11. He named things like people jumping out of windows, people crying, people dying, and the like. Then I told him what I saw. I saw first, that I was not on that plane from New York to Los Angeles. I had been previously upset because I had missed a screening of one of my films in New York and would have been on the plane to L.A. that crashed and killed everyone on board that morning. However, the grace of God did not allow me to be on it. I then explained what I saw when I finally started answering my phone that was ringing off the hook. I saw people so covered in soot that I couldn't tell who was Black, White, Chinese, Hispanic, or any race. I saw people helping each other. I saw people in compassion with one another from different races, caring for each other. I saw people in other countries across the world lighting candles and creating altars for those lost in the World Trade Centers and surrounding areas. I saw Arafat giving blood. I saw children praying for the lives lost in America. I saw flower dedications around the globe in remembrance of the tragedy.

Were I to believe in a God that he described, I would expect more mayhem in the Universe. But the God that I believe in is a God of Compassion and of Love. That God so loved me that it let me see this tragedy and know that there was something greater at work. This is the same God that I saw during the tsunamis. The God that is so loving that It caused troops headed to war to be deployed to the countries where the tsunamis hit to bring love in the form of food and to restore order in the form of compassion. Even these tragedies enabled me to know that God is unconditional love. It enabled me to see that not being in my loving is unacceptable. So, if I need to see my oneness with Hitler, then I too can know that anything that is in my behavior that is in fear, and not in loving needs to be released. If I think that I can destroy another in any small way – whether by gossiping or by killing, by seeing someone as less than or by seeing myself as superior, then it is that identity that needs refining. Because if I am indeed made in the image and likeness of God, I am more than this, as the lyrics of the Byars/Beckwith song say.

A new video game was released several months ago. This video game emulates the Greek wars. And it's called God of war. There's a great deal of excitement about this game. And I think that it came from how we glorify war. After all, we must believe in a God of war. When we look at the religious wars that have taken place, we don't have to look back to the 16th century wars between the Protestants and Catholics. We have things today, for example:

- In Afghanistan, there's the Al Quada (which ironically means The Source) and it is the terrorism taking place between Muslims and non-Muslims;
- in Bosnia, it's between Christians and Muslims;
- in Kosovo, it's between the Serbian Orthodox Christians and the Muslims;

- in the Middle East, it's between the Jews, Muslims and Christians;
- in Northern Ireland, it's between the Protestants and Catholics;
- in the Sudan, Christians are being crucified and people practice slavery;
- in Sri Lanka, it was between Buddhists and Hindus

Perhaps it was not the god of war that brought the tsunamis but my God of Peace. And I think those directly experiencing the tsunami must have felt something similar to those who fight in war; fighting for his or her life. The truth is there is only one God. Even if we take a polytheistic perspective, all of those gods came from one. There is only one Life. Even though there are many manifestations of Life, there is only one source. So whatever separation ideas we have are in our minds. There is really only one war. That is the war between separation and oneness. There was the war in Tibet between the Chinese communists and the Buddhists that exiled the Dalai Lama and the Tibetan monks. This was a blessing because it allowed the Dalai Lama to have a presence in the rest of the world that we may not have otherwise known. This spiritual leader stands for oneness. He stands for peace. He has the global heart.

Thank God for the Dalai Lama. And even as we use the term "Thank God," there's an implication that God is something outside of us. What are we thankful for, most of the time? Usually, we are thankful that our lives as we have known it have been restored to us. Thank God, I got my check that came today. Thank God, I got my son back from Iraq. Thank God I got my tests results back and they were negative. Usually it's because we think that God wants us to stay the same. But how could God want that when it is impossible. God Itself is ever unfolding and expanding. So, we have no choice but to expand.

Jesus the Christ gave us an opportunity to expand. He is sometimes referred to as the Lamb of God. In John 3:16, it says, "for God so loved the world, that He gave His only Son..." Yet, I don't agree that God so loved the world, because the world is effects. I think that even though humankind is part of that "world," it is Its own Spirit that God loves. And I think that God so loves Itself, that it created us in Its spiritual image and likeness so that It may continue to love Itself even more. But we got this idea from the Hebrew Bible that God wants a sacrifice. And we got the idea from the Christian bible that God wants it to be a human sacrifice.

Were we to really honor God in our actions, then it would be an act of faith. Otherwise, it's just an act of fear.

I'm afraid that I don't always honor God in my actions. It probably sounds strange for a ministerial student to say that. However, it seems to me that ministry is a constant walk in faith. Faith, as I see it, is about trust. And to trust in God includes a devotion to Good. But sometimes I get so distracted with what people say or do, presumably, "to me" that I don't see how God is using these same people to expand me.

During a difficult time in my life, I got upset with a couple of people. Both of them were accusing me of being either stupid or untrustworthy. Both of them were accusing me of being out of integrity. I took offense because I had some energy around each of them. I was indebted to each of them for one reason or another. I became angry because I felt I was doing the best that I could. Yet because I had been too embarrassed about what they would think about it, that I didn't take the time to let them know what was really going on. It became an opportunity for me to stand in my truth. I could have adopted the belief in what they said and looked at myself as a failure. One close relative could not believe that I could even consider such a thing. She thought I was the one that she looked to for positive thinking. And if I couldn't maintain, how could she. But it's not necessary for us to look to someone else for our Power. There are some who have been called a man of God or a woman of God who let us down in some way. It is not the behavior of a leader who has the yardstick for measuring good. It is our Spirit within us that knows.

I offer to you to look to that for your Power. Look to your Spirit for the Truth. Ernest Holmes' basic philosophy is that there is a God-Power at the center of everyone's being, a Power that knows neither lack, limitation, nor fear, sickness, disquiet nor imperfection.

Let's presume that that is true. Let us presume that as a fact for us scientists to prove. Let us test the idea of Wholeness and see that what we can do together is greater than what we can do alone. Look at our wholeness in responding to the tsunami. Are you convinced that there is a God? Are you convinced that God is for you? Are you convinced that God is powerful? Are you convinced that God is Infinite? Are you convinced that God is Perfect?

If you are not convinced like I am sometimes not convinced, I beg you to look at God another way. Like the student that saw fear and death, see

Love, Compassion and abundant Life. Like the brutal dictator that he saw, see the military dictator giving blood. Like the people jumping out of windows, see the people jumping for Joy in God. Like the religious wars, see the war within you between separation and oneness. Heal it.

Holmes also says that healing is not a process, it is a revelation. And he says that revelation is through the thought of the practitioner to the thought of the patient. He goes on to say that the process in healing is the mental work and the time it takes the practitioner to convince himself of the perfectness of his patient; and the length of time it takes the patient to realize this perfection. Are you convinced?

Take the time to sense God's Presence, to believe in it, and to accept Its completeness.

There is a power greater than you in the universe, and you can use it. Go ahead. Use It!

911

911 is a call
to report an emergency.
It's a matter of life and death.

Life and what?
Death. Death.
Does that word scare you?
Do you think you'll live forever?
Not even for a day.

For in a moment, this very moment
change is happening.
In this moment, I am dying
to the me I used to know.

I cannot, will not stop my death.
There's nothing I can do.
What God wants me to be
is something very new.

Something fresh – yet wise
from my life before,
something I'm evolving through,
something so much more.

Will you fight the death
when the moment comes?

Or will you surrender to the Life
that brings a possibility
to be more God, to be more Love,
to be more You?

9-1-1 is a call
to report a crime.

I'll have to make the call.
Not to report your unwillingness to surrender,
not to report your fear,

I'll call the God within your being
asking it to nudge you.

It may show up as a song.

And however it shows up,
your death has come and gone.

Fooled you.
You didn't even know it.

Now, what was it you were so afraid of?
Life or death?

CRASH TEST DUMMY!

"I wanna be a crash test dummy!" How often do you hear that statement? Maybe...never? Because crash test dummies are here so that we don't get hurt. They're made, in our image and likeness, so to speak, so that we can see all the ways that we could get hurt – if we were crash test dummies. That's kind of the way we do our life, isn't it? We play it safe. I wear a helmet when I ride my bike. I wear it so I get the feeling of security. I can be free to ride my bike because I know that, if I fall, my head won't bust open when I crash to the ground. That way, I have a sense of peace. We're perfecting our bodies – as if our bodies were our lives. But we know, in Truth, that our bodies are the temples of Spirit – the true life. And we respect our temples as a way of keeping sacred our true Life. We don't want to sacrifice our life as some say Jesus the Christ did. And it's really a peculiar phrase – when you look at it at face value from a Religious Science point-of-view. I mean, Life is eternal, after all. Right? What might be more accurate is that he sacrificed his body.
I looked up the word "sacrifice" in Webster's dictionary. The first definition was " to offer to a god or deity in homage," etc. Sacrifice means to give honor to God. The <u>second</u> definition is "to give up, destroy, permit injury to...for the sake of something of greater value." The third – to sell or part with something at less than the supposed value, to incur a loss. The fourth - a baseball hit to advance a runner. Most of the definitions seem to be something done in order to do something greater. Even the definition that speaks of incurring a loss is suspicious to me. Because I, an inquisitive one, want to know – what would make you give up something – if not for something else.
So I think we've got this whole living/dying thing mixed up.
I looked at my friend the other day in Intensive Care all hooked up to machines, monitors and the like. And knowing who she Is – and it is transparent that she's here for God – it became clear to me that she was balancing between the human love on earth and the Divine Love beyond. And since we're both Libras, I could relate. We're always seeking balance. But what a choice! To live for a family and friends who clearly and dearly love her or die to live with the awesome Infinite Love of God!
I was grateful that the choice wasn't mine. And then I realized that it was

exactly my choice. Who am I living for? How am I honoring God with my life?

Ego can keep us trapped in body consciousness, which is really experience consciousness. You know, it seeks to hold on to experience. To paraphrase Ernest Holmes, the founder of Religious Science, almost always our negative reactions to life, our unhappiness, and most of our physical disorders are based on unhappy experiences that are buried, but buried alive, in our memory. It can have no real existence of its own today other than as the lengthened shadows of yesterday. Whooh!

I wouldn't wear my bike helmet if someone had not experienced head damage in the past. And I'm not saying not to take precautions to preserve the body temple. I'm just saying, "How are you living?" Are you living not to die? Or are you dying not to live? Because it *is* a matter of life and death.

Breathing on our own is not living. It's a body experience. Jesus the Christ said "I have come that you might have life, and have it more abundantly." Is there something you're willing to give up in order to know more Life, more Joy? Is there an experience or set of experiences that is keeping you from living? Are you walking dead – or as they say – "Dead Man Walking?" The body is going to die. But right now, while it's living, how can you give it a good ride? A ride in Spirit, a ride in Life. I wanna be a crash test dummy! Because I'm willing to go through an experience and know that I'm going to live. I can know that whatever happens to me in the process can never destroy me. I'm a dummy because I'm acting as a tool for God. It doesn't mean I'm a stupid person. I'm the dummy partner. My life is exposed for all to see. I'm a dummy. You can look at my hand and plan your next move. Or you can simply be a tool for God. You *too* can be a dummy. And know that there are no tests, but refining. There are no tests, but proofs of Truth. And the crash? The crash is the collapsing of the illusion of Power that you thought your experiences had. There are no crash tests. There's only a Life to be lived.

Are you willing to live? Are you willing to let old experiences die? Are you willing to live free in this moment -- free from the lengthened shadows of yesterday? Are you willing to honor God with your Life?

I invite you to look at your life as the treasure that it is and be free to live. Be free to love. Be free to be a tool for Love. Be free to expose your life to its own Joy! Honor God. Honor Life. Honor you.

AGAPE

I walked into the honored space
knowing it was a spiritual place.
Down I sat in the pew
I knew I had some prayin' to do.

One spoke of God in human terms
then there were smiles, not frowns or squirms.
Hugging and holding were terms of relating,
no propaganda, protocol or baiting.

Songs of praise filled the air
words were spoken tender with care
Black, White, Red, Yellow and Brown,
many shades were all around.

Tissues were handed to hold the tears
of those who had come to release their fears.
Those who came had found peace
so away went the tension and came the release.

Allowing room for the Spirit to fill
the empty space with inner zeal
A blonde, brunette or red-head died blue,
God had made us in every hue.

Each shining brightly the magnificent light
the kind that makes a beautiful sight.
The Creator's gift of love
distributed among us from not just above

but within us and through us as we each give a kiss
to the child within us and it spreads like mist.
For once we go to that innocent spot
that space we were in before we were taught

hatred, jealousy or fear
or 'ere an ego to hold dear

before we separated one from another
or saw beyond the concept of sister and brother.

When we were spirits following the path
without frustration, bigotry or wrath
we were just children of the One
from whom we were given the sun

to show us the powers that brilliance can bring
and gives us a reason to sing.

So as we stand
holding another's hand
we recognize the strand
connecting man and

Woman gives birth anew
to another spirit or two
like a drop of dew

on a blade of grass
we can pass love on to last

another season
for no reason
but to find our way
to Agape.

DO YOU UNDERSTAND WHAT I AM SAYING?

Ernest Holmes, the Founder of Religious Science and Science of Mind, reminded us that Truth cannot belong to any one individual, but because of Its essence, It must belong to anyone who uses It.
I remember the first time I went to a Religious Science church. It was Founders Church and it was early in the 1980's. I went with a girlfriend and it actually didn't matter where we went, I was pretty much happy to be with her. I think that accompanying someone or bringing someone to church is kind of a special bonding event. The service was somewhat impressive in terms of its production values and there was some power in the speaker but there wasn't a connection there that made me want to return. However, there was something there that was interesting that I couldn't identify.
So it was understandable that, the first time I had invited my mother to Agape that it was hard for her to make the connection. The fact of the matter is, it was a little embarrassing for me. I had made her the subject of the flower dedication. She had made great strides in healing after a bout with a couple of back surgeries and the loss of her mother. And it was a particularly openhearted time for me as I was getting steeped into the teachings of Science of Mind and had caught a twinkling of the call at that point. Though not quite sure what to do about it, my enthusiasm was nonetheless high particularly for my spiritual community.
It had never been my intent to shakabuku anybody (the Nichiren Shoshu Buddhist term for trying to recruit people into their religion). However, I was certainly interested in having my loved ones understand what I'm interested in and exploring. I would have to admit, in retrospect, that I probably did have a little of the "my religion is better than yours" arrogance. Thank God for unfoldment and wisdom being a process, huh? My spiritual teacher, Reverend Michael, fully caught up in his message, posed the question "Do you understand what I am saying?" And my mother yelled, with equal volume as he, "No!" I tucked my head and tried to convince myself that this had not just happened. "Well, I don't," she said to me. This had not been the first time of feeling this feeling with my mother. I won't even share a similar instance when I was in a specially invited industry audience live stage production of "Six Degrees of

Separation" when she apparently (obvious to most people there) caught her first glimpse of a sex organ of a Caucasian male.

Thank God for unfoldment and wisdom being a process, huh?

The next year, a few weeks after 9/11, my mother came to visit for my birthday and my aunt came with her. She was now somehow a veteran and proceeded to let my aunt know who Reverend Michael is and share everything she knew.

So I knew she was paying attention more but not quite sure how much. Now mind you, over the years, I had been scoffed at by relatives about using words like "manifesting" and the like. So, I learned to measure my conversations and be freer with family friends who were familiar with New Thought.

Her friends started asking me for prayer and I started praying for them more and they convinced her that I had some healing power.

When I graduated from Practitioner class, she started asking me how I knew certain things and I referred her to some readings while I went off to the graduation party.

I think at some point, I figured that Religious Science was just my religion, they'd be where they are and I'd meet them there. So, the other day, my mother says to me, in response to something that I was having a challenge with: "Well, we'll keep saying it until it manifests. I'll throw it back at you." To which I replied, I was just meeting you were you are. And she said "Don't talk down to me. That's like talking baby talk to a baby. How is he going to learn to talk? You let me talk up to you." I was quite surprised by it. I had no idea the influence that I had. I've realized that Religious Science and Spiritual Truth cannot belong to any one individual, but being Universal it belongs to anyone who uses It.

THE EVOLUTION OF THE NUMINOUS

My personal experience of the numinous is continuing to evolve. The insights that I have gained in the last few months have expanded my concept of God. When I now mention God, It becomes more inclusive of the historical human psyche of all times. I understand the human need to create gods who personify certain qualities such as wisdom (Hermes), love (Venus) or Dionysus (ecstasy) or any of the other mythological figures. I also understand to a certain extent how these figures have become archetypes. One can try, by isolating a certain quality attributed to a certain god to commune with the divine in a way that is contributing to daily living. I understand how we have come to icons such as the Virgin Mary (derived from Ishtar of Ancient Babylon) and how today we have associated her as our connection with the divine in Catholicism, for example. Each of the saints personified in art portraits today carry a light around them which seems to be indicative of the energy of the divine. The mythological story of Osiris and Isis gives us the license to move forward through our own metamorphoses from falling to a death of a certain life to being reassembled and being co-creative as we lend ourselves to plant the seeds of a new order (which Horus represents). This story of Osiris and Isis reminds us that even as life as we know it breaks down and ceases to be (i.e., through the death of a relative or the end of a relationship), that this is a process of life reconstituting itself in a new way. As we experience a dark night of the soul, even in the torment we know that transformation requires these steps. This alchemy that the Hermetics used to derive the divine from matter is the same end that we all seek. The Neo-Platonist may have used theurgy, the Kaballists may have used symbols, and the Gnostics use sacrifice, but each one is identifying with the experience of the divine within himself or herself.
In the collective psyche as the temples of old were destroyed, we came to know ourselves as temples with the indwelling God beyond any external trappings. And yet we carry these same archetypes of old today in our psyche as we attempt to make sense of our lives. Even Christmas is a remnant of the Mithraism of old. We carry on the tradition of bearing gifts to the child of God. There is something within us that wants to give deference to the Divine that we perceive in others.

We also want to give deference to the Divine that we perceive in ourselves. So even if we don't give ourselves permission to do so outwardly, we may do as the woman did in her dreams by seeing Christ as a woman. She somehow was acknowledging herself as the Christ presence. We may not even allow ourselves to know that we can receive the love and safety that God has for us. Yet in a dream, the person saw herself kidnapped by brutes and she was (through a sort of Tonglin meditation) able to receive the love of God from above. With her embodiment of this love, she was able to love her captors and inspire love in her captors who let her go. We must find *some* way to experience God.

Whatever we may have inherited from previous generations in terms of symbols and icons are not limited to the good. We too somehow give ourselves permission to be Set (the ancient Egyptian god) and destroy someone out of our own insecurity. It may have been Augustine's attempt to isolate this archetype by labeling it "original sin" and making evil something we need to be saved from in our lives. This further justifies the importance and significance of needing a savior. We may even at some level see our enemies as our saviors by doing something to activate the salvation. One must sin, after all, before one becomes saved.

While we look to the depth psychologists to see how this may have played out from our childhood development, we can see that underlying all of this is the need for love. I know that God as Love shows up in all of Its creation, but we first look to our parents for that connection. When we do not get our early needs for Love met, the intense feelings magnify that need. The child, at the mercy of these feelings that contain terrors and needs eventually become the agents that separate him or her from other people.

I have seen it in my relationships early in adulthood. My parents' divorce somehow created a fragmented sense of self because of this external splitting. I see it in others, who may have had similar traumas, for example, of a sick parent who could not meet their early needs. I understand how this could turn into a pathological narcissism where one makes one's self the center of the world. Because there is not a normal relationship between the personal self and the transpersonal self (God), there is a psychological problem which may be seen from a religious point of view as a moral difficulty.

What is called "evil" is not something to be understood by a psychologist because it is a theological perspective rather than a psychotherapist viewpoint. While theologians see sin as deviating from the will of God, it is difficult for an objective person to know and definitively say what the will of God is. I understand, on a visceral level, that to unconsciously follow collective standards may be considered evil from a psychological or truly spiritual point of view. I have sinned myself by following what the norm said to do rather than being true to my Self.

It is understandable, therefore, to see how diverse different religions perceive evil. While the Hindus see evil as illusory without any separation in the all-ness of Brahman, the Buddhists see evil as the outcome of cause and effect and promote detachment; there is an inner value that is being challenged in some way. Somewhere in the thought patterns, we make choices against what is for our highest good. It could be by divine design. There is the perspective that there must be evil in the world in order to allow choice. Yet it is difficult for people to blame evil on the Divine. So Satan becomes the personality responsible for the evil. So when looking at this illusion of Satan, we see in mythology that Satan is the one who will not let the status quo rest. Satan is the one who incites rebellion. Satan inspired Judas. Yet we know that, without Judas, the salvation story of Jesus could not be complete.

I then begin to see that the rebelling that I do is to make myself conscious. Whereas Satan's primary flaws are pride and grandiosity, there has to be an impetus to balance this out. Looking at the origin of the word "Lucifer" which means carrier of light, I can see how this internal conflict is essential to the development of consciousness. This is what occurs for me when playwriting. There is a battle going on that must lead us to a greater understanding. It is probably this same idea that prompted the writing of the Upanishad story of Mahabharata where the battle is not for the purpose of harm but for restoring order and expanding the sense of the divine within.

We can deal with this shadow through humor on a mature level and allow an understanding of others to develop. If, however, I repress my anger, I may not be able to convert it into a way of helping others. When I recognize my personal shadow and admit that the face I want you to see is not my whole face, but the lighter portion of it, then I can form an ethical behavior that is not based on collective standards. I can embrace my personal shadow as part of the larger archetypal shadow and partake in the transformation of the Transpersonal Self. It is this Global Heart that I can heal.

It is interesting then to truly see suffering as a by-product of the "evil" that is an ingredient of transformation. While I needn't dwell in the suffering, I can identify it as a means by which I grow.

God, in Its Infinite Wisdom, uses all for the All. God, in Its Infinite Love, supports us through each choice, knowing that our inevitable Good is at hand. I am grateful now to be able to know on a deeper level what it means to say "Life is good - all the time."

GOD

You are wind, rain, sun.

You are that which moves, refreshes and lights

the world that I know.

FAITH

The *Science of Mind* states that:

> Faith is a mental attitude, so inwardly embodied that the mind can no longer deny it.

There has to be this kind of approach to life in the mind of a Practitioner in order for her to realize Truth for herself as well as for her client. This approach inherently comes from a philosophy that there is no end to what God will do for our highest good.

Although one who has lived in or through a great deal of challenges or pain may find it difficult to grasp this kind of philosophy, it remains the truth. Even in the face of physical or emotional pain, there is a benevolent Spirit that is aware of a Divine Plan for my life. For me, there has been a growing trust in this compassionate, loving Spirit. And it is this trust that has been expanding within my awareness. It is this trust that I can continue to nurture.

Ernest Holmes also stated that:

> We have to have the same **faith** in what we teach and practice that the scientist has, or the gardener has, and when that great simplicity shall have plumbed and penetrated this density of ours, this human stolidness and stupidity, this debauchery of the intellect and the soul, something new and wonderful will happen. It is the only thing that will keep the world from destroying itself....

This "density" that Holmes speaks of must have something to do with our ego where we allow our thoughts to look merely to the realm of effect and not to cause. This ego carries the idea that we are personality and separate. This could not be further from the Truth. The truth is that we are unique in our expression of the qualities of God yet we are one in God. It is God that creates the newness in our lives. It is God that is Life so Life can never be destroyed. Thank God for God because it is Infinite and because I am one with it, I am infinite.

Ernest Holmes also said that:

> When we train ourselves to use our mind affirmatively, we are choosing to operate in faith and knowing. And it is this faith that makes everything possible. It is the lack of faith that curses us because we see narrowly and in limited ways. Because I have listened and allowed myself to be open to the voice of God, I have allowed myself to be present with Truth. By this, I mean that I have surrendered to my will and said, like Jesus said, "Not my will but Thine."

The reason that I know that this works is because of what I have experienced in my life. There have been times when I have allowed myself to surrender to God and the miracles have occurred through my writing. I have been able to create because God is Creativity Itself. When I allow myself to sit in the stillness and listen to the voice of God, I simply follow and, as I am guided, brilliant things occur. I know that I am merely a servant. I am not minimizing who I am. I know that God needs me to be a place in which to express. But I have faith in God and know that "it is the Father that doeth the work."

I know, in times when I am not being creative but simply screwing up things in my life by not being responsible, that God is making a way for me. When I couldn't pay my rent, I surrendered and God provided the money. When I was in despair about my friend's suicide, I asked for prayer and it was God, through my friends, who helped to restore my faith through their love. They were allowing God to express Itself through them for *my* highest good. And, I'm sure, for theirs.

I know that when I had to face a large fine in Court, when I surrendered, I found out through friends who heard my request for prayer that there was another way, that it could be cheaper than what they represented to me. I trusted and followed that suggestion and saved hundreds of dollars! When my old car was falling apart and I didn't have the credit or the money to get a new one, the financing manager found a way – merely because of my pronouncement of faith!

When I had no way to pay my note for my new car, there became a way for me because I surrendered to God and others helped me clear my immediate threats to survival so that I could use the money that I did have to pay my note. When I asked for prayer for my cousin and I asked friends for support, things shifted for her in such a way that she is back to doing normal activities. By saying yes to this teaching, and coming into practitioner training, I realized the source of my false beliefs about money and prayed for abundance and asked for support. I even gave up my apartment and didn't have a place to stay and trusted. My classmate came up to me and asked if I knew anyone who needed a place to stay. This could only be God. And even though I thought I could catch up on my financial responsibilities by renting a room, I never dreamed that I could be in the company of consciousness people in the process!

When I found out that my office was closing, I continued to stand in my faith and they gave me a severance package that allowed me to live almost a month after I had to leave. The vacation time I "couldn't use" because "I was too broke" to afford airfare, is now cash to me.

I know that I can continue to stand in Truth and that even my greatest dreams can be realized. I have seen much adversity and challenges where my dreams are concerned, but I believe, if I continue to deepen in my awareness of Truth that I can continue to *really* **know** that all things are possible.

Life can only get better.

I AM NOT HELPLESS

I am not helpless.

I have God as my arms
my legs
my mind
my heart.

I have all strength
that there is.

I have all power.

I have all knowing.

I am the light.

I shine the love of God
in your direction.

I spread peace like
hot butter
on your soul

by simply smiling
at you.

THE FATHER'S GOOD PLEASURE

> Fear not, little flock; for it is your Father's good pleasure to give you the kingdom.

The Holy Bible, Luke 12:32
One of the ways in which my biological father showed his love for me was by giving me money. And he seemed to think that this was a demonstrative way of showing his care for us. I would venture to say that regardless of how he may have complained, that he took great pleasure in giving.
I used to perceive my father as being hard to please. So whenever I received praise, I was a little tentative in receiving the compliment. I wasn't sure that it was really for me. I think that a lot of us are like that with God. When we receive a blessing of some kind, we are a little hesitant to receive it. Are you sure you meant me, God? Ministers, can you hear me now?
I think it has to do with our old habits of putting our good outside of ourselves. Or, better put, seeing our Good outside of ourselves. And yet it is available. Most of my work is grasping that – on a continuous basis. There are times when I absolutely know that I am entitled. There are moments when I do not question that the kingdom is mine. And yet there are other times when I feel hard-pressed to go to that kingdom within. But it was my father's smile when I walked into his room at the long-term care facility a couple of weeks ago that has restored my faith. After being hospitalized for three months, he was moved the day before to a new facility and I was the first familial face that he saw. I could carry that smile with me every day now. So that even when I think that there is anything wrong, I can remember the feeling tone of his smile.
It is my father's good pleasure to give me the kingdom—in more ways than I know.
My father gives me everything that I need, beyond what I am expecting. I accept the kingdom now. I accept my Good now. I look for it. I expect it.

THE WELL

I have arrived at the Well.

It may or may not matter how I got there.
Yet I don't know that I should drink of it.
I am too innocent at first.
Then, too proud.
I am not equipped.

I stare at the Well.
It is appealing.
I thirst.

They give me water yet I am parched
for it is not from the Well.

They dunk me in the water
and I am cleansed on the outside.

My inside begins to seep out.
I release the shackle.

I am no longer a slave of the world.
I have touched the Hem.
I have caught a glimpse of His mercy.
Her Love is elusive.

I cannot grasp it but I am honored to be the object of Its Love.

I have followed the footsteps to the Well
and it is safe to be here.

I lower my ladle to drink of It
and It is Peace.

I lower myself gently into the Well.
I immerse myself in It inch-by-inch.
I am transformed.

YOU GAVE US LIFE

You gave us Life.

How can I understand
the crazy thought
that make the children kill one another?

You give us Love.
Where does this self-hate come from
that causes bullies
to feel your strength
by stripping another
of his self-esteem
of his Self
of his God-
consciousness.

How can
a child of Yours
not feel Your Love,
not know Your Peace,
not know the Joy You have in store
for each
and every one of us.

How can
a child
not know
how special he/she is to You,

how much you long to
hold her/him,
to touch her/his heart
with
Freedom

to Love
to laugh
to be
everything
that You designed
her/him to be.

How can this wall
that seems to separate
the children
from the Light
be
destroyed?

What must I do?

Not him,
not her,
not them
or You.

What must I do?

GOD AND THE WORLD

Sometimes, as we cultivate our spirituality, we think that we need to protect our consciousness from the world. And the Bible does say to keep watch. But in so doing, we may tend to separate the world from Self. We *are* in the world and we don't know how to be *in* the world without being *of* it.

We won't even watch the news because we don't want to see the war or the pain. The fact is that there is no separation. God is always in the midst of it all. But it's hard to see that when you're in the gap of separation. For instance, to look at the killing, I can see the effects of barbaric behavior and think that compassion is missing. Were I to look deeper, I may come to know that this is the part of me that needs healing. Just as we realized after 9/11 that there is nothing outside of ourselves, that we are all one, so we must know this always.

In our relationships, we think that we need to protect ourselves from our family or our special someone because we feel as though we are under attack. This is really an opportunity to see how violent we are to ourselves and to others. Yes. I am guilty. I don't always eat right. And at times I'm not so kind. But God is still right where I am. I can be compassionate with myself as I release the pain and harmful behavior. I am the change I want to see. And since I am one with the All ness of Life, this must be true for everyone else. So, in truth, there is no God and the world. There is only God in the World.

I am compassionate with my self and with everyone else because I am one with the All ness of Life. There is nothing outside of God.

THE HEART'S HUNGER

When we think of the heart of something, we usually know that we are talking about the center of it. It is the heart that will drive us. We may not always respond to it. But that something within is that truly pulls us is indeed our heart. God is that heart, that center, the core of our existence. And God is always calling out to Itself. It is part of the loving activity that God is. God seeks to reveal Itself. Just as we seek to reveal ourselves. We may use terms like "I am trying to find myself" or "I don't know who I am" or "I don't know why I'm here." There is something within us that wants to know ourselves better.

Yet all we really want is to be loved. Well, God is Love. So we just want to experience who we truly are.

According to the thesaurus, heart is also synonymous with spirit or mind or compassion. Spirit is what we commonly know and identify as power, courage or will. It's a force within something or someone. Isn't it? When we attempt to describe a person in a eulogy or an awards banquet, we are often referring to the substance within them that causes them to accomplish much, love much, be a wonderful caregiver or humanitarian, a dedicated teacher or a model citizen. It's the spirit of the person.

Heart is also synonymous with mind. The heart longs for more of itself to be realized. It longs for more love, more peace, more joy. Doesn't it? This longing is for spirit to be realized, recognized. Our attention or our consciousness is on what is really Real to us, what is important to us or what is necessary more than bread itself. This mind is perception. It is how we look at the world. Our perceiving through a certain kind of lens, as it were, creates what we experience.

There is an inner knowing of what is genuine. And the core of our being is faithful to that, dedicated to It! That is why Ernie says that we long for it. It is our very Wholeness because it is God. And God is All there is – Wholeness itself. In knowing God, I know all. So Religious Science in its core concepts elucidates, reveals, explains, expounds, illuminates life. Ernest Holmes, the author of <u>Science of Mind</u> and the founder of Religious Science took the essence of the great world religions and philosophies and scientific proven facts to support the one basic premise of all life – that we are the thing Itself.

It is the awareness of our oneness that is truly our salvation. It is why we embrace the Global Heart vision. It is because we know that there is truly nothing outside of ourselves.

God is Love. We want love. We are love. Once we know that what we want is what we are seeking with, we need look no further. We can release the desperation of wanting to find our soul mate or someone who can make us feel whole. We can find it within ourselves.

God is Prosperity, Abundance, sufficiency, Harmony. We are chasing money because we think it is something to get. When all we really need, we already have. We are Prosperity. What we are seeking is the trust in God that lies on the very dollar bill that we are grasping to acquire. Were we to trust our very core, our Essence, our truth, we would know that all of our needs are already met.

So the more we can embrace our oneness in God, the greater the quality of our lives. Ernest knew that this teaching of revealing the Self to the self is the answer to the release of all human suffering, sense of loss, angst and pain. He knew that all of these experiences that we think are real are not. And that we can choose to know our highest Self. And in so doing, free ourselves so that true joy may be realized. This is God's will.

PEACE

Oh, mercy, mercy me.
Forgiving can be hard to be
And yet I know there's none outside of me.

Mother-Father, God, love them through me please
for I cannot do so with ease.

Beloved Spirit, I rest in thee. I seek answers to set me free.

And I know Truth can be found
when I listen in quiet, without a sound.

We turn within to be in Peace and
allow all thoughts to cease.

HOLY ONE

Fear not what is not real, never was and never will be. What is real, always was and cannot be destroyed."

- Bhagavad-Gita

Recently, while singing the opening chant at a healing, revealing service, I remember getting a very clear vision of an Israeli suicide bomber. On a cellular level, I sensed that this spirit was a holy one. I know that he thought of himself that way. He connected with me in that moment as if he was singing the chant. I neither invited him or expected him. And in the midst of my Knowing, I knew that he was a holy one. It felt like a male energy and it was a committed, sacred spirit.

It may be easier to judge any of the people sacrificing their lives and killing others as maniacal or diabolical. It is only at the level of spirit that we can see one another and understand each other in the midst of their pain or in the midst of our pain. What may seem obsessive to us could actually be an intense interest in loving God.

There are many questionable things that have occurred over the millennia in the name of God. And I have judged them as hypocritical or political, as a strategy of power or a selfish ploy. But somehow in that moment, I understood his holiness. Somehow I understood his dedication. Would that I would have such dedication to my spiritual convictions. Would that I would have the kind of faith that I can stand in courage despite my fear.

I know that there are many events of today that seem to come straight out of the Upanishads battle in order to unfold a greater awareness of heaven on earth. Yet I have noticed a few things about me. I am motivated less by seeking my own personal desires but more by fulfilling a need to be here for God. By being on divine purpose, I am assured of being authentic to my self. And by living in this truth, I am also safe and protected -- no matter how crazy my actions!

I live to be in communion with God as all life and I am supported, protected and enriched because of it.

I AM YOUR VESSEL

I am Your vessel, God
I am Your tool.

Mold me in the shape that would most serve You.
Breathe the energy in the direction in which I should go.

Fill my mind with thoughts of creativity
expressing You
expressing love
expressing life
expressing joy
expressing peace
expressing freedom
expressing light

Fill my heart with love
so that I may show
what God looks like.

I am Yours.
You are mine.
We are One.

I live to be Your expression
I am Your courier
for Your message

I am the instrument for Your light
I AM OPEN, available to Your guidance.
I am complete through You.

There is no me without You.
There is no anything without You.

You are everything.
I praise You!

I ask You for a word.
And the word You gave is joy!
Oh how precious You are
to give me that most precious gift -
the one gift that only You can give
because You are Joy itself!

I am filled with gratitude
for Your grace
You give me joy.

Joy is Spirit
and I simply open my heart to Your will
and that is Your only desire.

Is it Your joy that I feel
and not mine then?

It makes no difference
We are One.

I CAN TURN ON THE LIGHT

Before God did anything else, God said "Let there be light" but God created the sun and the moon much later. This makes me think that this light is the beginning of being creative. And as I apply it to myself, it seems to be giving permission to myself to create. And the light may be, in fact, knowing that I am a creative being -- **really** knowing it and being able to step into it.

The light basically sheds those illusions about "I can't," and those tapes that maybe the family said, i.e., "You can't make a living doing that. It's not practical" or an industry saying "that's not commercial" or whatever those other can'ts are. Eric Butterworth says it is the fear itself that creates that thing that gets in your way.

It is clear that the light truly dispels the darkness. The darkness is not accepting the good, not accepting the kingdom, not accepting the gift, the life that is my very own. So, yes I can turn on the light so that I may see my own creativity and be that which God designed me to be - in freedom. I'm willing now to acknowledge the fear, without giving it power. I am willing to be all that I am, beyond anyone else's ideas of my limitations. I am willing to "divide the light from the darkness" so that I may truly see Who I Am.

At this time of new beginnings and the celebration of new life in the Spring, I embrace the Life that is within knowing It is my Power. I look inside during this season of Lent to know that I and my Father are one. I celebrate with Purim that creative expression of letting go as I let God. I am now willing to let the Light that is within me shine.

SURRENDER

I sit beneath the pine trees.

My eyes rest on the mountaintop
as the clouds usher in the sun
until the Light expands to fill the skies
with Its brilliance.

The butterfly -- no longer cloaked
in its wings of shelter --
rests on the ground. It seems to have
surrendered to its death.

I turn away in sadness
and allow the crickets to serenade me.

My eyes return to see the butterfly has gone.

It found its flight in Its surrender.

It lives – beyond the visible –
eternally.

INDEPENDENCE

In John 10:30 in The Holy Bible Jesus the Christ said "I and my Father are one."

In-dependence Day is what we call the 4th of July. And, because I love words, I sometimes take them apart to play with them. If I look at in dependence, it would seem to be something limited, something that is needy, unhealthy, blah-blah. However, when I realized that there is only One thing to be dependent on, I knew the truth. And for me, the truth is that when I am in dependence on God, I can relax. When I am in dependence on God, I can take a leap of faith. When I am in dependence on God, I am supported. When I am in dependence on God, I am safe. And I don't know about you, but it's very important for me to feel relaxed, to be in faith, to be supported and to be safe. And the wonderful thing about being relaxed, trusting, feeling supported and safe, is that I am free to love. Hello. And that's all I'm here to do.

I've been creating in one form or another all of my life. And I've always known that I wasn't the source but there was/is a source that is available to me whenever I decide to make time to come to it. It is plentiful. It always has enough and then some. I can depend on It. It will write through me. It will express through me. It will love through me. It makes me look good. And it certainly makes me feel good. It makes me wonder why I don't hang out there more often. Because when I am in dependence on God, I am free.

Jesus the Christ, the Way Shower showed us that the way to be free is to depend on God. Amen.

I am free for I am One with God. Together, we co-create my joyful emancipation from darkness to Light. It is a revolution into Love.

HEALING

The pain.
The pain is not in vain.

The ache you feel
is very real.

It may seem like the end
but it's the means
by which you will bend

and transform and weans
you away from fear
of getting near.

Embrace it.
You can't erase it.

Don't swallow it.
It won't pass.

Don't wallow in it
or it will last.

KEEP COMING BACK. IT WORKS

I remember a joke about being addicted to coffee. It talks about all of the ways that you know you're addicted to coffee like when you can jump start your car without cables, or when you answer the door <u>before</u> people knock.
If you can imagine what it must be like for those people you work with or those family members who have an addiction, you would have to ask "What if you had that kind of commitment to God? Knowing God as your source, you could know that your energy is Infinite and you *could* jump start your car, without the use of cables. Heck, you could allow the currents within you to do any number of things.
Were you to – not merely believe – but truly know – that your mind is the Knower's Mind, you would not only answer the door before the knock, you'd probably answer the phone before it rang or send an e-mail to someone simply by knowing what the message is they were sending you. Sometimes we refer to it as synchronicity. Sometimes it's just "by right of consciousness." Whatever you'd like to label it, It's Omniscience. Many times I've called someone and they've said "I just mentioned your name three seconds ago." Or someone will tell me they caught something in meditation and went to their computer only to find an e-mail from me about that very thing. I absolutely know the oneness of God. I count on it. And you can only get it from communing with Spirit. You've got to keep going to the Source or perhaps I should say – keep staying with the Source since It is right where you are.
It is the commitment to praying without ceasing. When it is your foremost desire to commune with Spirit, you are on vigil for opportunities to see the face of God. And you keep looking – because you know when you see it, it's going to be good. When I go into surrender mode, I'm able to let Spirit write through me. I let Spirit's Creativity have its way with my imagination and I am truly amazed by what comes through me.
And It's energizing. It's absolutely energizing. I find myself sometimes with an unlimited reserve to serve. Family and friends look at me with concern, pleading with me to get some rest. And I'm being pulled by a vision that won't stop until It has used me to do what It needs to do. And

more often that not, it's usually an exercise in opening up my own heart's awareness to myself.

So that when I think of myself, I think of myself in terms of Spirit. When someone says "How are you?" No matter how I'm feeling, I can say "good," because I know that there's Something in me that is Good. It is Spirit Itself.

Now, even when I get angry or frustrated, I'm looking for the blessing. Something within me starts percolating. A friend cancelled on me the other day saying that she wasn't going to be good company. It bothered me because I was really looking forward to seeing her. But then compassion kicked in and I wanted to make sure that she was all right. It was important for me to allow my emotions to lead me to a greater Truth – an understanding beyond understanding.

Remember when you just wanted a date or a relationship? Well, now we all seem to want to be with our soul mate. It can't just be a romp in the hay or even a committed relationship. It has to be soul mate (or a twin flame, or the like) – because this person has to resonate with your Spirit. Once you realize that you are a Spiritual being, you find that you are meeting people at the level of Spirit.

Because God is with me everywhere I go. Not just in the shower but in the dirty, nasty places that I go in my mind. It is ever asking me to look for the Spiritual Truth of any situation. It is ever finding opportunities for me to heal an unresolved source of pain – to dispel a belief in something other than Truth.

So I have to keep coming back to God to re-charge my battery. I have to rely on the greater I Am. It's a co-dependency that makes my life work. It's my relationship with Self that I have to keep coming back to – because It works. Keep coming back. It works.

GOD IS

God is
the bird's song
the man's whistling,
the sunrise,
the children's laughter.

God is
the writer's poem,
the singer's song,
the dancer's dance.

God is
hands holding,
eyes connecting,
legs jumping,
you smiling.

God is
a kiss on the cheek,
a meal on the table,
a chair to sit in,
a breath breathing.

God is
Life.
God is love.
I am love.

God is
I am.

KNOWING HOW TO LIVE AND

KNOWING HOW TO DIE

Knowing how to live seems to be a daunting task. We seem ill equipped to know with certainty what to do in order to live life in a way that gets us the results that we want. Perhaps it is the expectation itself that brings the disappointment and frustration.

As Stephen Levine talks about in his book that he wrote with his wife, Ondrea Levine, "Embracing the Beloved," we have a mold into which we pour our reality as those ideas of who we think we are. These models are the ideas of the Truth, not the Truth itself. And the attempt is usually to fit our lives into these little pre-prescribed molds. Well, our lives don't fit. Because we are one with the One, we are ourselves Infinite in our expression. It is the human tendency to try to fit the largess of Life into a smallness that makes us ill. How could it not?

When we resist because we desire things to be other than they are, we cause our own suffering. Yet when we accept life as it is, we are at peace. Why then don't we just stay in peace and accept life as it is? I submit that it is the lack of acceptance that is the seed for growth. Were we to be satisfied with life as it is, we may never explore to be more or to expand. Our expansion would only come from an inner activity that is introspective. It would be a slower one, I would think. It may not be what Suzuki Roshi calls living life like a very hot fire, because there could be the distinct possibility that would be a trace left behind. Yet there would be no doing but exclusively being.

It is that life of being that is the life of peace I want to realize. I think that knowing how to live is knowing how to be. Just be. So much of this keeps reminding me of the poem, "The Invitation," by Oriah Mountain Dreamer, that helps me to realize that peace and know the living life as a hot fire for Self, for All.

This, to me, is a description of how to live. For example, to risk looking like a fool for love, for love is the only reason for living. Touch the center of your sorrow (which sounds like grief to me) and you *stay* open. That's living! To sit with pain without trying to fix it is being! That is truly being fully alive!! To live is to not be afraid of joy either. To really live in the wholeness and abundance without fear of limitations is to be alive! It *is* about being true to your Self. It is about staying in integrity in the face of betrayal. That's the God stuff that I want to embrace! To see the Beauty when it's not pretty is to be a practitioner, to have the knowing of the Source as my life. To know that in the midst of the disappointment (or seeming failure) and *know* that Good awaits me is **truly** faith. That's knowing how to live. To continue through my own grief to be there for those who cannot do for themselves is to be practicing the Presence. That's being alive! To love myself through the empty moments is to know God, **really**.

Once I am living from this space, I cannot fear death. Death can take nothing away from me. It is only another transformative event that leads me to more good. And, the best thing about it is even if the worst thing happens to me (for example, death), God is still there. I am never alone. That's why I can see that there is no difference between knowing how to live and knowing how to die. When Levine talked about finishing business, he was talking about keeping your heart open and seeing the oneness of all life. There is a knowing that cannot be robbed by death. If we continue to just be and not resist, we can die with grace and dignity, knowing it is simply the beginning of a new adventure.

If we can die with this attitude, surely we can live with this same quest for adventure!

I should like to die to this self so that I may know this full life of adventure right now!

THE SACRED HEART ASCENDS

The Center of All Life is the heart of knowing.
The heart beats in celebration of Its Joy flowing.

Infinite Peace imbues Its being
while intuitive Light makes for right seeing.

Beyond illusions of fears and woes
and acting out conflicts –

the One Mind knows.

Together, we're a composite of the one Mother
here to support and be kind to each other.

The One Life expresses in so many ways
and human life is just one phase

of expanding Itself in Love and Compassion
while effects consciousness receives Love as a ration.

Beyond the senses, Spirit awakes as you
And Life is revealed as fresh, vibrant and new.

Creativity thirsts!

Passion bursts!

Life releases Its Power
this hour

in delight of Soul –
always Whole

responding to Love's call
in deference to the All.

This moment. This now -

unconcerned with how —

the heart is free to be
both she and he
both thee and me —

in One

Eternal life transcends.
The drama ends.

The sacred heart ascends.

LOVE: THE BRIDGE TO DIVERSITY

Some scholars say the Book of Ruth was written in the fourth century Before this Common Era. Due to the practice of marrying foreigners in another country, some scholars say this story must have been written during the periods of Ezra and Nehemiah as acts of rebellion. Jeremiah had already told the Israelites to get over the idea of being separate and simply marry the people where you live and build communities and wealth. But the prophets Ezra and Nehemiah made it clear that it was unacceptable for a Jew to marry outside of the race. All who were married to foreigners were told to divorce, leave or return their children to the mother's family and marry a Jew. They were told to start again with their race as a sign of solidarity and to reclaim their faith and customs that had since become diluted.

Naomi was heading back to Judah. Naomi told her widowed daughters-in-law, Ruth and Orpah, to return to their homelands because they no longer had any obligation to her. She kissed them and they cried. They both said that they would return with Naomi to Naomi's people. Naomi said why? I don't have any more sons to give birth to that could be your husbands. God will deal kindly with you as you have done to my sons. Orpah agreed to leave. But Ruth clung to her and refused to leave with the famous words, "Entreat me not to leave thee, or return from following after thee: for wither thou goest, I will go..." Ruth had made up her mind to stay. Ruth did not have to be in exile. She was free to go in the physical, external sense. Yet her heart would not allow her to go. Naomi's love was not something she could release. Ruth stayed with Naomi and because she did, she later wed another kinsman of her former husband.

We cannot help who we love. And regardless of what the civil laws may say or what society's taboos may attempt to dictate, we do marry outside of our economic class, our race or our faith, or even outside of the heterosexual margins of man and wife.

The Book of Ruth is a perfect example of how love leads us and pulls us. We know that God is Love. So, indeed, it is Spirit who is pulling us. It is Spirit who is guiding and directing our hearts. Our spirits know when we are being called to a greater vision, a greater purpose, a greater fulfillment (including fulfillment of prophesy, if you will).

Ruth did not know that she would be a maternal figure in the lineage of King David or Jesus the Christ. Yet her son was the grandfather of David. She simply followed her heart. I have an Aunt Ruth like this.

Some of us don't always go by the rules and simply follow our hearts because we want to be in our joy. Ruth was like that. Ruth was clear about what she needed to do.

Ruth symbolizes the love of the natural soul for God and for the things of Spirit.

We know when we are following Spirit, it is different from following our rationale. Ruth went where love led her. She loved in the highest degree. She was loyal and her devotion is indicative of spiritual thought that brings its own reward.

She didn't follow after men or money. She simply followed her spirit. Thank God that there are people who have intermarried with other cultures. Although Hitler and other purists would frown on such things, it is the diversity of people that brings cultural beauty. America, this country, is a melting pot that has brought together many cultures. We have all found ways to preserve some aspects of our culture and regain our heritage. We have all found ways to appreciate the differences of one another. And we have found the Way to know what is alike in all of us. As we have become more tolerant of living together, we have learned about each other. As we have become more loving, we have reaped the benefits, just as Ruth did. Ruth became an ancestor of the anointed one. And I'm sure she had no idea of this when she simply trusted love.

She had a connection and that connection was more real to her than anything in her past. Naomi and Ruth were linked together. They had a rapport, a relationship based on mutual respect, cooperation and friendship. This is the kind of love that we all seek. It is a love that allows you to be free, to go about your own life. And if you choose to be in a union that is close, it can become a partnership. And a partnership in its most ideal form is one that is mutually nurturing. This is the kind of relationship that Naomi and Ruth had.

Now some daughter-in-laws and mother-in-laws do not get along in this way. It may be that they are concentrating on having first place with the son/husband or it may be that each woman wants to feel as though she is the powerful one in the family. Whatever the reason, this kind of in-law relationship is one of separation. Ruth chose not to be separate. Ruth chose the association and the closeness.

When we are free enough to choose something different, something unpopular or something even forbidden, we are taking a risk. When people intermarried prior to the 1960's, they would be the victim of at a minimum, derision; at its worse case scenarios, they would be found hung, shot, stabbed or in some way, dead. When homosexual relations were discovered, people were beaten and/or arrested or killed.

However there are people who have chosen love for love's sake. Those who have taken the risk have sometimes found misfortune and grief. Yet those who stuck it out and remained loyal (like Ruth) have reaped a great deal of joy, abundance and love.

Were it not for love, Martin Luther King, Jr. could not have succeeded in bringing people together regardless of race. Were it not for love, Jesus would not have been able to talk about a good Samaritan (an oxymoron in that day). Were it not for love, we would not have the diversity in this world. Were it not for love, we would not know the possibilities of tribes merging and alliances being formed. Were it not for love, there could not be a United Nations. Were it not for love, we could never know peace. Were it not for love, we could not know life as abundantly as we do now.

UNCOVERED

Love does **not** equal pain.
Money does not equal pain.

Love is here in support of me.
It comes in many forms.
I am free to see Its face.
It is indeed abundant in its grace.

And I am *full* of gratitude

The blindfold is gone.
I need not stumble around,
creating illusions of what might be
there to hurt me.

My eyes,

uncovered,

see what is Real.

Freedom is home, at last.

LOVE IS KNOWLEDGE

Parker Palmer quoted St. Gregory in his book, "To Know As We Are Known," saying that the more one loves the more one knows. This quote convinces me that Love is Truth. It's impossible to find God without being in God.

Some of us believe in evil. Even though we Religious Scientists profess *not* to believe in evil, we do. Any time I acquiesce that I am lacking, I send bad thoughts to the Universe and it feels like evil is conquering me. And the more I believe it, it is so.

The Christ said that it is done unto you as you believe. This philosophy enabled him to be a healer. Believing this phrase fills the practitioner's prayer. I have prayed and seen its effect on the person for whom I was praying. There is an acknowledgment of the Presence that is unspoken yet palpable.

How could it not be that the Lover knows?

It was a challenge to look at the proponents of war and not see the transgression of greed or a lack of compassion. It was a challenge to accept that President Bush truly was on a mission from God. It was a challenge for me to accept that any of us are not terrorists because we are all guilty of scaring each other. We have all told someone that the conduct that he or she was doing was detrimental to him or her or even to the planet.

My Professor's response to my question of "how do I find the love?", was to do an exercise looking for love. It was a wonderful experience of being kind on purpose to everyone. It enhanced every conversation. I felt joy-filled. I was excited to be alive. I found in them what was already inside of me. I was looking *with* what I was looking to find. And my experience of receiving it expanded! I continued to know Love as I loved.

I look for Love and I find it within me. And I also find Joy, Beauty, Creativity, Harmony, Compassion, Freedom, Wholeness and Peace in the process.

NIGHTMARE AWAKENS

I laid in a room of darkness
in a bed of loneliness
on sheets printed with despair
covered with a blanket of longing.

tossing and turning around in my head
the merry-go-round melodies
of an unsuccessful love affair.

Over and over it played
on the turntable of hysteria,
while the ears of my soul bled with grief.

Climbing over the barbed wire fences
that kept me from happiness,
I escaped from the dream of no rest,

opening my heart's curtains
as the Light of Your Love
shone through.

THE LOVE KNOWN 'ROUND THE WORLD

The Book of Psalms is abundant in describing spiritual knowingness. This book has been spoken of in terms of religious experiences, but it is my belief that once something is known, it is far beyond something as fleeting as an experience. It is commonly believed that the Book of Psalms may be used more than any other book in the Old Testament and perhaps it is due to the fact that the Psalms are expressions of faith. Rabbinical literature refers to the Book of Psalms as the Book of Praises. According to *Old Testament Light*, the book of Psalms contains messianic prophecies.

Most of the Psalms are attributed to King David and were later written by court scribes. Some are believed to have been written during his early youth when he wandered on the hills of Judah in the desert feeding sheep. A poet-musician, David spent many hours alone singing, playing the harp or lyre and composing new songs. In his solitude, David knew the glory of God. Psalm 22 is described in the King James version (the Open Bible Edition) as a cry of anguish and song of praise. It is believed to have been written by David.

The consensus seems to be that the author wants to know why God is so far from helping him. The people of that time (much like some of us today) were impatient when prayers are not granted immediately. We would rather die than be left to live in our grief, oppression or persecution. It is doubtful that anyone really believed that God has forsaken them. Certainly Jesus, purported to have uttered the same words, knew this (although, according to the Aramaic expert, Rocco Errico, the true Aramaic translation is: My God, My God, for this was I born). Of course we all know as Jesus did, that God never forsakes us - even those who seem to have gone "astray."

David is saying that we get impatient when our prayers are not immediately answered. But all that is necessary is that we trust God, who is able and can do all things. God is abundant Life, inexhaustible good. Even in my weakness, something inside of me knows that my good is always available. Regardless of what the world says or what appearances may suggest, there is Courage and a Wisdom within me that is simply the grace of God.

It is God's grace that gives me this wisdom. It is God's Love that fills me.

God is so good. God is so compassionate. I am thankful that it is God's Life in which I live and have my beingness. My soul surrenders to that inexhaustible good.

I thank God and praise God that this Spirit within me, as Christ so magnificently showed us, is that upon which I can always rely. It is the Substance of my life. And it is my Oneness in God that sustains me, maintains me, nourishes me and lifts me all the days of my life.

I am so grateful that God so loves me that It remains with me. I am so grateful that God loves me even in my times of doubt, worry and pain, even in the midst of my turmoil. God is with me always.

Christ knew this and showed us the Way. Praise God for Its Love, for Its Good, for Its mercy, for Its Compassion. Praise God that I am that I Am. This is powerful stuff. Perhaps this is why the Book of Psalms has universal resonance known by people all over the world.

WHAT A LIGHT YOU ARE

What a light you are

what a joy it is
to listen to you speak to my heart and soul
and remind me with each thought that God is
my strength, my hope, my everything
that I could ever need.

It's really faith that we speak of.

Even the desire in my heart came from God
from the start.
My love, my abundance, my art
are all from the One.

But, oh, how I long to see me as you do
without worry or fear,
just the strength of God and the knowing
that all my dreams are here -
not far away or another day
or even out of reach.

The way you love
the way you hold me
is the way you teach.

You see me in the light, not dark
and you show me the way
into my mind, my heart, and my soul.

And everything is fine.

My gratitude for you is great!

A new life has begun!

Cause God used you
to heal my fears
and remind me of my power.

The truth within is that
I do nothing at all.

I merely open my mind to see
the way to listen well
to what God says and reveals
through my heart and my head.

My soul is deeper, higher, wider
than it has ever been.

It's the love of God
in your helping hand
that's cleared away the fog.

I love you.

I thank you.

I know you.

You are one with God.

A MOTHERLY LOVE

You, when you know that all you do of good is done by My Spirit, also know that to keep a conscious oneness with that Spirit and its Power, you must drop from your life the negative thought and thing.

- Eva Bell Werber

Whether you take the Bible literally or figuratively, I can see where Truth is revealed in the story of Moses, as an infant being first hidden, and then placed in an ark of bulrushes, slime and pitch and then being placed in the reeds by the river's brink. It speaks to Motherly Love not only in the heart of Levi's daughter who placed him there but in the heart of Pharoah's daughter. The Egyptian mother paid the Hebrew mother to nurse Moses and bond with him. How good is God?

It speaks to the feminine principle of Levi's daughter as the Soul, the Womb of Nature, impregnated with Divine Ideas. The idea of compassion sits within her so grounded in her being that she cannot bear to destroy her child because everything within her says - more life!

So regardless of the Pharoah's edict to throw the male babies in the river, the child lived. It is because the Holy Mother within both women was receptive to the Spirit of Life. The Holy Mother gives birth to the ideas of Life. She is the key to the Creative Process.

This story allows me to pay homage to the feminine principle within me that says yes to all Good. No is not an option. Because it is only yes that affirms Life, affirms Love and affirms Joy, I say yes to Life. And more life is revealed! It's that simple.

Happy Mother's Day!!
Praise Love!
I say yes to Life. And I say yes to Self.
Then the floodgate of Good opens to shower me with Love.

AT HOME WITHIN

I have been asked in
quite a bit as of late.

Happily I consent to go on
the brief yet full date.

I'm not taken anywhere away
but right here at home I would stay,
not in my living room or even my bath
but where I go is on my own path

into the quiet, the joyful serene,
the only location where Truth can be seen.

Beyond closed eyes and darkened rooms,
beyond scary ghosts and deserted tombs

into the space of eternal abyss,
into the face of perpetual bliss.

Embracing the quiet,
erasing the riot
of struggle and strife from my mind,

escaping the diet
of negative thoughts that entwine
the present and future with the past,
for time itself doesn't last.

So in the now
I make a vow
that has no boundaries of space,
that has no quandaries of race

consciousness on which to rely,
lot or cautiousness to deny

acceptance of All.

For there is nothing outside of the all.
It's Within.

And in there is no with Out.

There is no out.

So rather than seeking something outside of self,

I'd rather be being my Self.

I'm home, always home.

I am at home within.

MY NUMINOUS LIFE

My image of the Divine is an ongoing evolution. Gone are the days that, in my early childhood, I could even allow the image of the old White man with the beard to be the all-and-all of my life. Even as a second-grader I couldn't buy in to an angry God who punished babies for something called sin for which they would go to purgatory just by virtue of the fact that they were born and died before having been baptized.

While I matriculated through undergraduate studies, I came to the conclusion that the clergy who had represented themselves as intermediaries of God could not, in their corrupt activities, truly be informed as to what Truth really means. Thank goodness that things happened to open my eyes to the possibility that an inward journey could most effectively serve me with a direct connection to the Divine that is indisputable.

I had, after all, come to that conclusion when I was somehow compelled to attend church every day in Lent during the seventh grade. It logically made no sense. I wasn't the best behaved or necessarily most respectful of children. It had to have been the numinous that was calling self to Self.

I was baptized a second time in the pool behind the Baptist church in Pasadena. I had no recollection of my initial baptism as an infant in the Catholic Church. But after having been in the pool at the Baptist church, I was somehow cleansed internally for there was such a magnificent gratitude for the compassion of God and the Love of Jesus, that I was deeply moved.

I have, however, had remembrances of a moment during my First Holy Communion when I had a real knowing of what a sacred occasion it was. I remembering wearing white and very few other details outside of the remnant purse that I received on that occasion that contained the picture of Jesus on the sacred heart, the rosary and the veil for my head. Something had happened there and I can easily access that moment as well as the moment following my second baptism – almost on demand.

As a writer, I have had many numinous experiences. The most magical ones seem to have been in my poetry and play scripts. Something obviously had taken over and had brilliantly created characters and/or put together words in a way my mortal brain as I knew it could not have fathomed. Still and all, it took me a few decades before I came to the conclusion that it was not I alone that was doing the writing.

Coming into Religious Science was as inexplicable. Although I knew I had made a conscious choice, the choice itself was less pronounced as was the experience of being there. It had to have been by Divine Design that I had arrived there.

It was not until I moved forward into the religious science classes that I came to realize that I was not simply there by command, but that I had made an agreement (in consciousness) to be there. It was during that time that words began to come out of my mouth that I had no knowledge of knowing before those moments neither what they meant nor why I had to say them.

These numinous experiences increased. And as I stayed in surrender, Spirit continued to lead me to certain books, to writing certain poems, essays or later, talks and to being sensitive to other realms outside of the physical realm. It was the silent yes that kept compelling me forward. And even as I remained unaware of how powerful it made me appear, I remained just as open to letting It have Its way with me.

It has led me to a commitment to the Ministry which continues to keep me befuddled. And yet, I somehow know even as my resistant mind efforts to talk to me of my unworthiness for such a calling – that this is how Divine Order would have it.

In this adventure of ministerial school, I not only continue to realize my divinity but the many faces of God that have preceded me.

The mystics, in their attempts to articulate even one chapter in the Bible, cannot even begin to touch the 'hem of the garment' of the Presence for words fail to serve in that manner. The depths of understanding that I have come to know in those rare moments of reading scripture with clarity and wisdom can scarcely be remembered. And yet the radiant Truth that did occur will be with me always.

Even as recent as yesterday or this moment, I am blessed with the knowing that at any second, a healing (facilitated by Grace) is mine. For in the Divine Pattern, It is ever seeking to reveal the wholeness of my Self to my self. I am grateful.

THE SLIGHTEST RIPPLE

Just the slightest ripple

tells me that Life – not loud

is quiet and perfect.

MY SOUL IS A WITNESS

> The truth of religion does not depend on tradition nor historical facts, but has an unerring witness in the human soul.
>
> - George Ripley

When studying the sources of New Thought, I discovered a group that flourished for a time called the Transcendentalists. This group looked at intuition as the basic source of the knowledge of reality.

I found this to be intriguing because I consider myself to be a budding mystic. In that, I mean, I am one who is becoming more and more reliant on my inner compass than any external facts.

Truth is such a personal thing that it evokes our passion and confirms our knowing. It is the thing upon which institutions, countries and even wars are built.

My soul takes whatever I discover in the realm of the senses and guides me into an awareness of Reality that is deep. I have given consent for this to occur on a level that remains conscious but of which I am unaware on an earthly level. In the process, I go to a place that is rich yet indescribable. As all that I am resonates with a certain spark of light, it is as if another brick is placed on the foundation of my Spirit, building the house of my consciousness.

I am grateful to know that my house has no roof but continues to expand in Truth. My soul is a witness.

It is enough that I have gone to the well and drank. My soul is fed and I am refreshed.

My soul, as compass, knows how to lead me there any number of times in the course of a day. I am simultaneously able to function in the external realm. But it is my intuition that leads me. I would like to think it will lead me more than my ego or mental arrogance. I would like to be that kind of transcendentalist.

I joyfully follow as Spirit guides me in Truth to ecstasy and knowing. I accept my Good. I embrace my Life as Wholeness, Perfection and a harbinger of Truth.

INFINITY

The great connector
of life,
the ever-present
Essence that Life is

I think Your thoughts
I share my fear
and You are there
answering

in the form of Ancestor
in the form of Truth
in the form of Abundance.

You shift my focus
from darkness to Light,
from inside
to outside

from single
to All.

For
Infinity.

THE NEW MILLENNIUM UPANISHAD

In the Bhagavad Gita, there is a story of a young man in the midst of a great war. The battlefield is the setting for the sermon that Sri Krishna, the embodied divine, the guru, gives to Arjuna, the warrior, who is distraught about the possibility of killing his family and friends. I understand how Arjuna feels. Sometimes it seems as though I am in a battle against my family who has old ideas of convention that don't jive with my spiritual journey. I don't want to hurt them but I must be true to myself.

In the field of the Kurus – the Dharma-khetra – the battle is not merely an external battle, a battle for kingship, or power or land, but an inner battle, a battle for Dharma. This Dharma stands behind and guides the unfoldment of this scripture and of this battle which is called Mahabharata. Krishna, the divine incarnate is an avatar. He can intervene and bring about certain changes. He explains to Arjuna that one must give everything up to the divine, and when one adheres only and supremely by the divine, one finds that the divine law manifests itself consciously and dynamically in us. The law that is unfolded in this battle is the law of Sri Krishna. I experience this as my consciousness is unfolding as well. I have surrendered as I become more of a ministry. And in surrendering, God acts through me. I have no will greater than the will of God. It is my power and I rely on it. I no longer seek my desires but the unfoldment of good, which is undoubtedly greater than I alone could imagine.

The Hindu sees unfoldment during certain movements in which there is a certain kind of Dharma or law. During the Staya-yuga, truth reigns as heaven on earth. In it, every individual, every event and entity embodies and manifests some symbol of the truth. During the Treta-yuga, life is largely pure and perfect, yet it has a little impurity and imperfection. This imperfection multiplies and truth is eclipsed. Man, reaching for formulation of truth, falls from grace. During Dwapaara, an upsurge of darkness, truth is preserved but conventions are all important. (This is like the era we are living in now. People are tired of wars and don't understand why they are losing their family members for the sake of someone else's idea of terrorism or freedom.) Conventions can't be tolerated any more and there is a breakdown of the system. This system is breaking down now as individual countries refuse to unite (e.g., the EU), but look out for their own interests.

During Kali-yuga, the age of individualism, egos are rampant and all restraint is gone. It appears that President Bush's ego has gone rampant along with Dick Cheney and others who don't seem to realize the insults they are slinging across the globe carry their own repercussions. I fear that it will take a great war to restore us back to the golden age of fulfillment. Dharma will be restored, for it is always active. It is the law of truth. Knowledge is seen through the four Dharmas of man. One is the power of knowledge that is realized by a truth seeker, a bestower of knowledge or a sharer of knowledge who wants to bring truth into the world. Another is a warrior. Another is one who exchanges his consciousness for money, like businessmen. Another is the laborer, who is skilled in manipulating matter. The Brahman are like the preachers and the spiritual talk show hosts like Oprah or the writers of Chicken Soup for the Soul or the speakers like Deepak Chopra. The warriors are the militarists and the dictators who are the Kshatriyas of today. The Vaisyas are the corporations who will find a way to acquire money by any means necessary. They are creating a two-class system where the Suudras today are the lower class (usually minorities or immigrants) who will do the labor.

This consecration of intelligence, this pressing for knowledge and for true understanding yields to us the body of divine knowledge. This is what Arjuna is called to do. This purification of intelligence calls for us to draw away from the senses and desires and all things that attach us to the life of the body. We must make a distinction between the body and the dweller. Once we are purified, there is an active opening to something which is coming from above, a discrimination and an intuition that tells us how to choose and we grow in our faith, in our ability to understand and we embark on the path of true thinking. In this thinking, I listen. Out of the listening, I understand through a seeing, an intuitive vision, and from that, I enter into knowledge.

Out of the pure seeking after truth arises the light of true knowledge. I find that the more I seek truth, the more I acquire real knowledge and by knowledge, I mean growing into my identity with the supreme consciousness.

When I surrender to the will of the Divine, whatever is the Divine's will achieves itself more successfully. Moreover, as I yield the fruit of my work to the Divine, I loosen the knot of the ego. Self-interest is no longer part of it and a witness consciousness absorbs the action proceeding by a higher force that does what needs to be done. When I enter into the union with the divine will, my consciousness lies in the true light and wisdom and the motor parts and choices fall into union with the divine will. I make choices that are not what I had planned. I say things that are noble instead of the race-conscious mode I might have chosen were I not awake. The union of the witness and the union of the action is fulfilled as liberated works in the world. Krishna asks Arjuna to be like the Jeevan-muktas who are free even in the world. This is what I am becoming as I become less concerned with what others want and more concerned with what God wants to do for me, through me and as me.

Krishna identifies himself as the most powerful representative of the qualities and works in which its characteristic soul power manifests itself. It is in this form that the divine manifests in the world, as vibhuuti. Each one of us can unite with that god-power within and see our progress as the progress of God within us. Jesus exemplified this through his Christ-consciousness. In the lineage of Avatars, we have the blueprint of the evolution of consciousness. Each person's consciousness is aided at every critical step by a god-power that comes. We can each call upon the god-power within. And as Martin Luther King, Jr. found, there is a limitation beyond which the Vibhuuti cannot go. When the laws that hold together the world are questioned at their basis, there *seems* to be a decline of Dharma and an ambiguity enters our dealings with things so insidious that no one can say for certain what is true and what is false.

In those moments when I have known the vision that encompasses past, present and future co-existing all at once, I too staggered like Arjuna. The vision is inexplicable by human words. This enormous love seems like too much to take. And yet I am so grateful to have known it. The reality of the Avatar is that the Avatar is here to give a Dharma, a way by which one can grow towards divinity. In the form of Buddha, for example, he stands as the gate through which and the way by which men shall follow.

God gives of Itself so freely and unconditionally without asking for anything. It is in my consciousness, I realize that it is God who acts through me. It is my charge to use this knowledge and my work as a symbol of my love to God as God has done to me.

ROSE

Rose,
hiding
inside her bud
a shade of red
on pinkish tones,

She turns away
at first
from her richest color
to attract not the wind

which tears her apart from herself.

To open her arms

she dares not
for fear of embracing
a
hunk of snow
that would still her
into
death.

Instead,
she shelters her body
until forever

or maybe Spring

but
even then
her instincts fill her thorns with sharpness!

Roots
planted too
deep
to see
too close
to feel,

while
life pumps to her veins
with

VIGOR!!!!!

OBEDIENCE TO THE WHOLE TRUTH

Truth is universal yet how we perceive it is so personal. Whatever religion or practice we submit to may differ according to that perception. I can remember a time when I was taught that my religion was the only one that would get me to heaven. Yet my experience was that good people from other religions were showing me heaven here on earth.

Through my spiritual studies, I have realized that my personal truth is what I bring for God. Everyone's expression of his or her personal truth is an offering to the wholeness of us all.

My judgment about myself doesn't change my truth and my judgment of others doesn't change their truths. But when I listen to your truth, my truth is expanded. I don't need to compare myself to my old self or the self I want to be. So perhaps I can lighten up on myself where new year's resolutions are concerned.

I can be aware of where I am and continue to listen to the voice of God within me. That is my only mission. That is why I am alive. If I serve God in body as in spirit, I can be the effect and the cause. I need not question it or how I measure up to its perfection. The wholeness of truth requires me to be able to see my own perfection. How else would I be able to be It?

I just have to obey my truth the best way I can so that my power to live it may grow. I am compassionate with myself as I obey my truth as best I can in this moment.

That is obedience to truth, and that is, to me, to live fully. That is accepting Life. That is accepting Love.

I am compassionate with myself as I listen to Love's voice and obey It the best way I can.

IN AWE

It is beautiful and vibrant.
I am in awe of Its Creativity.
It is only God.

ONE MASTER

According to the King James version of the Bible in Matthew 6:24 –34, no one can serve two masters. The verses tell us that attempting to do so will cause you to hate one of the two masters.
This section is from Jesus' Sermon on the Mount. The "sermon" is on the mountain which, in metaphysical terms is a high plane of consciousness or a state of spiritual realization. Jesus the Christ is on a higher plane with the masses leading them to their own realization. Not only is he living in his Christ consciousness, he is embracing the Christhood in each of the people who have come there to know truth.
It is God that is his Master. It is God whom he serves and invites us to serve. Yet that God which we serve is hidden away. It is a secret. It is the mysticism that cannot be explained, yet must be courted constantly.
The other "master" is the mammon. A definition of mammon is treasure, wealth, or riches. The mammon is temporary. Mammon refers to the outer, formative world that is the object of one's desire to gather and to hoard. Mammon is the material or worldly thought and belief.
By keeping God in our hearts or collecting the thoughts of God, we are serving the true Master. Yet, more often than not, it is the mammon master that we pursue and revere. We are concerned, as indicated in Matthew, Chapter 6 verses 25 and 31, with having something to eat and drink and have clothes. And yes, our human survival relies on the substance of food and drink and our outer protection relies in part on our clothing (or raiment as King James would indicate). However, we are spiritual beings having a human experience. God is the very substance, life, and intelligence that is the source of everything that lives. It is the God substance that is real. So it stands to reason that it is better to serve that which creates what we want rather than the outer expression of it.
Matthew 6:26 tells us that the birds cannot reap or sow (like man can), yet God takes care of them. Yet I am under the impression that my being anxious or worrying about how I will be taken care of can help me or grow me (Matt. 6:27). It is the Father within that does the work. There is nothing I can solely do that could increase my stature. The lilies of the field grow without working (Matt. 6:28). They don't do anything but make themselves available to Spirit to expand through them. When

speaking of having thought for raiment, Matthew references Solomon in 6:29: "that even Solomon in all his glory was not arrayed like one of these."

Solomon was a pretty important figure to the Jewish people. They looked upon Solomon as being wise and peaceful. He was after all, the direct descendant of David. I'm sure referencing Solomon brought great weight to the people of that day. "When asked by the Lord what He should give him, Solomon chose wisdom above riches and honor. Then all the other things were added…" Solomon, the great Jewish king, chose the Substance of Spirit and all of his riches followed him.

As indicated in Matthew 6:32, "your heavenly Father knoweth that ye have need of all these things." God loves us and is always availing our Good to us. Were we to not worry and trust, we may find that we are, in divine right order, provided for and loved. It is in the letting go and letting God that we experience our miracles. It is the release that is necessary in order to accept our good.

Matthew 6:33 plainly tells us to seek first the kingdom and all things will be added to us. All we have to do is go to God, or go in God because God is within us. Why do anything but go to the Source? Why go retail when I can go direct to the manufacturer and get it wholesale? If I go to retail, I'll know I could have gotten a better deal in the wholesale market. It won't be diluted. It will be pure. When we release everything to God, we don't have to think that we have anything to do with controlling how our good comes or whether it comes.

Matthew 6:34 is as follows: "Take therefore no thought for the morrow: for the morrow shall take thought for the things of itself. Sufficient unto the day is the evil thereof."

We worry about tomorrow. And we need only to know that God provides. Just as the slaves from Egypt realized, the manna will always flow. To try to store something up for tomorrow is to presume that God will stop providing. If we are not living in this now, we cannot be free and we cannot be in our joy. For it is when we live for tomorrow, that we lessen the gift of today. It is in the now moment where we can best realize our good, our blessings, or the grace of God. It is in being present that we can know our divinity. It is the belief and the acceptance of God's good that activates the answered prayer. It is how the Law works. It is how we participate in the creative process, by simply letting go and letting God.

Reading or hearing the phrase "..for the morrow shall take thought for the things of itself" reminds me that thought is powerful and creative. If I am not in control of my thoughts, I may very well be misusing the law and inviting a whole set of dissonant experiences. So if I am going to exercise my thoughts, it may as well be about now - <u>this</u> moment. It would behoove me to focus on the creative power of thought and keep my mind stayed on God, now.

"Sufficient unto the day is the evil thereof" basically means that there is enough trouble to deal with today without even going to tomorrow. Even though some people think that metaphysicians do not believe in evil, a more accurate perspective might be that we know that evil is a result of misuse of the law. People concerned with effects bring about strife and confusion in mind, body, and affairs.

I think we may have some left over purity laws definitions of what a master is in our minds. The public opinion was that a master was someone who had authority over you and had the power to influence or command you to do something. Nothing and no one can have power over us unless we allow it. So we bought the information that a master is a judge who has or may have a negative opinion about us. So every time we have a negative opinion of ourselves, we think that God has a negative opinion of us. And it just ain't so.

Our God is so loving that It allows us to master It. It has built in us the power to activate our own good by simply accepting our good. Jesus showed us how God allows us to master when he washed the feet of his disciples. Jesus said that a master is no greater than his servant and a servant is no greater than his master, inviting us to serve each other. Indeed, whenever we serve God, we are serving ourselves. And vice versa. Whenever we are serving ourselves, we are serving God. And we are really only serving ourselves when we focus on the inner. We do not serve ourselves by focusing on the outer. The outer is not permanent. The inner is eternal.

It is a matter of how much faith we have. It is a matter of how much trust we have. It is a matter of whether we serve a little god or a big God. It is the big God that has all the power and somehow we may not think we are worthy of the big God. We are used to being enslaved in race consciousness that tells us that we are not good enough to receive our good. We have bought the lie that we are not worthy because we are sinners. So we serve the little god because that's how we see ourselves. After all, we know we are made in the image and likeness of God. Whatever our impression of God is what we accept for our lives. Within, we know the truth. We know that we are centers, not sinners. We know that we are the place where God resides. Were we to serve a little god, we would get little results. And we would resent God for having all that is available and not giving it to us. But we don't have to worry about that. Our good is available and accessible. Our good is within us. All that is required is to accept this and believe that God is God. The way we serve our master, God, is by waiting on Him. It is the way we assist God. The way we work for God is simply letting God be God.

SMOOTH

God is a blue

wave with a white cap

collapsing

on to the sand.

God is so smooth.

PURIFYING THE CONSCIOUSNESS

In a psychology class, I underwent the exercise of having a talk with an imaginary wise figure to help me to understand my feelings. I was able to become my own counselor. As I continued in my studies, I learned to work with my inner advisor in a way that has really opened windows, doors and cubbyholes that were deep and unknown to me.

I used the method of the inner critic to address a couple of my issues. One issue is being in love with someone which, of course, would not be an issue if I were sure the other person felt the same. I had enlisted my inner advisor to help me with courage in both my love life and my career. Somehow calling forth courage seems to enlist bigger anxiety in my life. In this instance, I followed it with the exercise of coming to terms with my inner critic. What occurred was more than I bargained for because I got into a space where I did not want to ask the inner critic to stop and I did not want to increase the quality of courage. I wanted to use the inner critic's pessimism to say that there's nothing I can do. I even allowed this feeling of helplessness to reveal a poor self-esteem. Although my critic has become less brutal, it did allow me to see my hopelessness. While I invited it to guide me in doing a better job next time, I had to ask the question of why I repeatedly fall in love with the wrong person. What was revealed was an underlying core belief that I am afraid that I can't have a successful relationship. While it was feeling awful and looking ugly, I had to allow myself to be gentle with me. When I thought about how I had sabotaged my relationships based on this belief, I also realized that I just have felt like a failure or worse, someone undeserving of love.

I realized that I had been tolerating the critic in order to keep me from facing responsibility and to save me from making changes in my outlook and my behavior.

I looked at how my inner critic had been keeping me in limited beliefs about my career. In getting a sober look at this on a visceral level, I know I have begun a journey of freedom in releasing my Self to my self.

I have a clarity now more than ever about how faith healing has helped me move through my lack beliefs in my financial affairs. And I see how my belief in my own deservedness and entitlement has led me to a greater acceptance of my abundance and prosperity as well as to a deeper commitment to order and management in my affairs. I will continue to use faith healing if ever those moments come again when I start to slip to slip into lack and limitation.

I used my inner advisor to guide me and counsel me in the area of my response to my father's health challenges. My Dad was hospitalized for serious health challenges consistently for months. I had to come to terms with being in loving and not in my judgment and being in surrender and not control. I needed my advisor to remind me about the wholeness and power of my Dad as a spiritual being and not as a fleshly being in strife. I now have permission to let me explore my psyche and to uncover unknown territories in my mind/soul.

YOU AND I

I see what you look like
as you sit in your chair.
Can't imagine what it feels like
cause I'm not there.

But I'm loving you and
being here
freeing you to love me
and breathe new air.

Lifting you and holding you
in my heart and hands
knowing you and comforting you
through your fear.

Though your doubt and worry
comes and goes,
know that all the while
God is loving you.

Know that all the while
as I smile,
I am God's courier
here to deliver the message

I am God's child
to touch you in Its stead.

touch your hand,
touch your heart,
hold your hand,
kiss your head,
tell you a story,

sing you a song
dance you a dance,
poem you a poem

dazzle you,
gaze upon your face…

Looking in a mirror,
I see me.
Do you see you?

SACRED MINISTRY OF LIFE

According to Joel Goldsmith in his book, *Practicing the Presence,* Nothing comes into our experience unless it comes from God.
Some of us look at service as helping others. Then, it becomes a great way to feel good about ourselves.
The illusion of helping others may lead to getting into what Ram Dass calls "The Helping Prison." This is when one "helping person" suffers judgment from being identified as "the helper." When, in truth, if we are alive, we are here to support life - regardless of what role we accept for the moment. Each one of us is a ministry.
Those who stay in service sometimes feel it is a burden or a task. So when I see this or I am this, I remember that it is not me that does the work but the Father within. Sometimes it takes a minute. But when I make the connection with the Divine in another person or another life form, it is clear. I am here for God. Period. That is sacred. That is service.
I surrender to the loving Power within me and I am Love; I am in service to Life!

GRATITUDE

Gratitude is a state of being
Gratitude is a way of seeing
what you have and what you feel.
Gratitude is a way of being real.

Gratitude is an attitude - a feeling,
a means to begin the healing.
For when you are grateful, you know
that you can't reap what you sow.

cause what you receive is more than you've earned
what you know is more than you've learned
because there are intrinsic gifts
that God built in to give us lifts,

give us smiles and give us laughter
that guide us to live happily after
what we perceive to be the end
but is really another bend

on the road to eternity,
another path to liberty.

Gratitude is an attitude that oft brings us to tears.
Gratitude is an attitude that allays some of our fears.

Gratitude is an attitude that helps us to see the light.
Gratitude is an attitude that helps us to know our might.

Gratitude is the true mirror of who we really are
Gratitude is the attitude that we shine like many a star.

Gratitude is the knowing that all is well.
Gratitude is the glowing that can't be felt in hell.

Gratitude is the point of view
that each day is new.

Gratitude is the attitude with which I end my prayers.
Gratitude is the attitude that tells me someone cares.

Gratitude is the attitude that God is present and near.
Gratitude is the attitude that there is nothing to fear.

Gratitude is the attitude that everything is mine.
Gratitude is the attitude that stops every whine.

Gratitude is the attitude that love is very real.
Gratitude is the attitude that I like to feel.

THE SECRET EXPANSION

At one point in my ministerial school training, I expanded internally and collapsed externally. I knew I had gone beyond the letter of the requirement but I believe the work I did was a good contribution. While my studies were deeper than ever, my tolerance for external criticism was shallower. I suspect it was an inner impatience with not manifesting the growth that I was sure was occurring within. But I certainly got an opportunity to grapple with my faith. It was all good and it was <u>not</u> all good.

A couple of years ago, I taught a number of concepts informally to teens. In an event for youth, we were seeking God's highest idea for our youth and family ministries. The youth were really candid about how much or how little they felt loved. The parents were authentic about how much or how little they practiced the principles at home with their kids. It was a blessing beyond the vision that came to me. I was floored.

Although I had experience in teaching and in working with youth, I still found myself intimidated by what I didn't know.

I had been struggling with expanding my prosperity consciousness. It was difficult for me to keep up with my financial obligations – especially after losing my job. It put me back in terms of my already late obligations. I was faced with the fears of my parents who were terrified at me being unemployed. My father challenged my sentiment that God would provide whatever I need. I had a truly dark night of the soul sitting with my fears. I did not shirk from them and it was ugly and painful. It seemed as though the night was darker than before. I was blessed with the sprinkling of love from my friends and that helped me a great deal. My class work in Pastoral Guidance was a big factor and some of my classmates in that class assisted as well. In that particular quarter, it was even difficult to see a practitioner (spiritual counselor). In addition to my financial concerns, I didn't want "help." I just wanted to be with where I was. It may have made it more difficult for me not enlisting the support of a spiritual counselor but when I realized how ridiculous it was for me to try to do anything without the help of a counselor, I started setting the appointments.

I was really getting epiphanies and deep revelations in my Bible studies. After four Bible classes, I began to have spiritual moments of real clarity beyond words. There was a reality in experiencing the Christ consciousness that was unprecedented.

There was a deepening going on and I became intolerant with some of my colleagues. I became weary of the jargon and I wasn't afraid to let them know that. I suppose I had some kind of uncompassionate ideas with regard to leadership and what I think it should look like for others. Even when we interacted socially, I was frustrated with their inability to see how clearly and definitely the Law works in our lives. Perhaps it was just my own self-bashing that I was doing and projecting on them.

I felt as though I should have been producing more results than I was based on the work that I had done. Although I was proud of my gains in my personal practice, I knew I had such a long way to go. So I grappled with my worthiness of being a ministerial student. I thought that I'm not spiritual enough to do this work. Who am I? And then I began to think that I cannot <u>not</u> to do this ministerial work. But I don't really know what that means. I did know that my speaking skills, my writing skills and my other areas of being creative can be a great asset to furthering spiritual growth in myself and, in turn, to others. And I did know that when I am in communion with God, miracles occur. This kept me on track. Were I not to have continued in ministerial school, I think this would have still been true.

I came to realize that my praying in secret is enough. It doesn't matter what I think of my own spirituality. I can, however, be more compassionate with myself. I can be less critical and release expectations of what I should be doing. I can be more self-accepting, which will aid me in accepting others where they are. And even if I feel as though my feelings are hurt or I'm not being respected, I can use the opportunity to expand in self-loving and honoring myself in different areas of my life.

If I start with where I live and beautifying that space, it would even be more honoring than being unhappy with it and letting it look however it looks. I would honor the temple of where God lives – the God that is me. It requires physical work in addition to the spiritual work. Yet, I don't want to concentrate on the physical of the process as much as I want to concentrate on honoring Self from the inside out. This may make it less of a secret!

WHEN I THINK ABOUT YOU

When I think about You
I am so full.

Your Love expands my heart
as a balloon --

sending me soaring

through stratospheres and
hemispheres and

right here,
right now.

I know that You exist inside of me

I am so honored,
so thrilled,
so humbled.

I am so very complete.

SUPREME LOVE

What a wonderful opportunity to smell the fragrance of my union with God. A couple of years ago, holiday trip to visit my family brought many gifts. My growth, my process and my seeds of Light were revealed through me. The ride from the airport revealed how critical my roots are. God as Compassion revealed that there are wonderful aspects of everyone to be celebrated from different ethnic backgrounds.

God loves me so much that God showed me my own impatience through my relative's impatience with different ethnic groups or with traffic. It felt violent but it was a wonderful opportunity to show me my relative as teacher and my role as healer.

And God didn't stop there, joy of a family member laying eyes on me allowed me to see the Light of God in her. How wonderful it is to receive the abundant love of God - the greatest gift.

I attended a Catholic church this particular Christmas Eve and I remembered the ritual of my youth. It was then that I came to realize after four decades what they had been trying to make me believe as a youth. It was all so simple but it used to be complicated. The story of a young man's giving ness to his family was illustrated as the love of Christ. Spreading the incense was less mysterious. I clearly knew that he was honoring this divinity, the sacred space and all of us. How great to know the intention of purity and honoring Spirit within all.

How good to know the real intention of communion is not to feel worthy but to know there is a constant communion. The fellowship of church is an opportunity to embrace God in each other. How wonderful to see the honoring of the Holy Family. How good it is to know the honor of every family just being together as God's Divine Plan.

I honor the Spirit within me and the spirit within each person for God is revealing Itself through our communion.

TAKE A VACATION

August is a popular vacation month. It's a time that a lot of people get away. I wonder what they're getting away from. For that matter, I wonder what we're getting away to. I don't think we can really get away. We can't get away from God. And God is all there is.
Perhaps taking a vacation is removing us from something, somewhere. I'm taking a vacation from work. I won't physically be at the place I go to daily. I'm not there. I'm elsewhere. I don't need a plane ticket not to be present. I suppose I go on vacation a lot. The more "vacations" I take, I realize that I'm not interested in being there. I'm not being fed there and I'm hungry. So I get away from there to get fed. I may rejuvenate my body by relaxing but what I'm really doing is feeding my soul.
I submit to you that in order to be present, you must go on vacation. It may sound like an oxymoron but it's true. I'm clear where truth is and where truth is not. We truth seekers may not make an announcement when we are leaving to find it. But we do go after it.
Vacate implies that there is an emptiness where something once was. In truth, that space was already empty and went to get filled.
So I invite myself to go on vacation more often. It will be a trip whether I leave town or not because I'll go to a place of adventure, of enrichment, of substance. I will have the time of my life. And even if my body is in the same spot, you'd better believe, there's some movement going on. I'm not there. I'm home.
I am present with God because I hunger for it. The emptiness will not sustain me. I seek It because I am It.

THE WAY WE WERE

For some reason, we have a proclivity for romanticizing the past. So when holidays like Memorial Day come up, we remember. We remember our veterans who were killed in the wars. We remember other loved ones who are no longer with us. And we remember the way that we were with them. Somehow, it seems as though things were better *then*. Somehow, we were younger, perhaps thinner, and more appealing. Now seems less glamorous, somehow boring and definitely not as grand – when we are caught up in the memories. After all, even that person is not here. How good can it be? "We'll never have another like him" or "those were the days."

We look at pictures and those with full heads of hair may now be bald or may have bigger bellies. Somehow, it is even easier to see our own beauty then more so than now. There is an uncredited prayer that attempts to enter into a compassionate space yet still is from a less powerful energetic. The prayer says:

> God, lift the hearts of those, for whom his holiday is not just a diversion, but painful memory and continued deprivation.

But I know that this life can be lived without prolonged pain. I know that every memory need not be painful. I know that we are never deprived of anything but ever expanding in our realization of Good. I know that there is an ever-expanding Spirit within each one of us that is beyond time and space. It is here. And it is now.

Memorial Day was established after the Civil War and was originally called, Decoration Day. Apparently, there is evidence that organized women's groups in the South were decorating graves before the end of the Civil War because a hymn published in 1867, "Kneel Where Our Loves are Sleeping" by Nella L. Sweet carried the dedication

To The Ladies of the South who are Decorating the Graves of the Confederate Dead"

This idea of where our loves are sleeping is what we failed to remember. We failed to remember that our loves who have gone to the other side are latent. And by that I do not mean that they are inactive, but that they are hidden from our mortal eyes. But even the woman holding the scales of justice is blindfolded. This ought to tell you that justice is blind. It is beyond the human sight. It is a God quality. Even though we do not have the physical body present to love, they are resting in the loving arms of God. They are quiet in the calm and settled breath of God. They are embryonic, emerging, budding, developing. Why would we want them to be anywhere else? Decoration Day is the name we should have kept. For when we are decorating, we are celebrating and adorning those things in the material realm that keep our joy alive, that keep our lives exciting, energetic and exuberant.

Decoration Day would begin to describe the honor, the respect, the credit, the tribute that we have for our fallen soldiers. It would then begin to express our love. It would then begin to express our appreciation, our recognition, our praise, our homage, our glorification of these our brothers and sisters who have gone beyond the realm of the visible into the Light of Love. So it would be love that we are expressing as we are remembering them. This is the same with any grief wherein we may feel that we have lost the opportunity to express our love for our beloved, although this is not the Truth as we know it. As a Religious Scientist, I am aware that I have the opportunity to communicate with the invisible. I have the opportunity to meditate and hear the voice of God. I have the opportunity to pray and evoke the Spirit within me, awakening my own spirit to the Truth of my being. In prayer, I have the opportunity to tap into my own dormant power, my magnificent knowing, my amazing loving. And yet as we remember our transitioned beloveds, we fail to bestow bounty in its proper place. We may bring flowers but we can't seem to recall that the invisible life is the real life.

Since the Civil War, there has been the Spanish American war where the U.S. was given Guam and Puerto Rico and bought the Philippines back from Spain for $20 million.

There were many wars that followed. There was World War I (that they somehow named The Great War [as if any war could be great], and there was World War II (which could have been great had we learned then to release our racist habits and tendencies) after having learned the lesson from Hitler. There was the Korean War where we somehow got the notion that we needed to end communism, from which we might have gleaned instead the value of cooperative economics and where we might have learned how to mature socialism into the Global Heart encompassing a world that works for everyone. There was the Viet Nam war where we made unification seem like a struggle instead of the natural awakening to our oneness. There was the Persian Gulf war where greed for oil overcame the practices of collaboration, compassion, forgiveness and cooperation. There was the Iraqi Crisis where the fear of weapons created an unreal and seeming justification for war. Now we are in the Iraq War where we seem to be somehow convinced that the fear of an axis of evil is real and that this fictional fight is somehow freeing us from our fears when we don't even have the freedom to just stop it!

Somebody needs to know that we are not here to glorify fear. We are not here to live in the past. We are not here to be afraid of the future. But we are living in this now moment. And in this now moment, we needn't think about tomorrow. I'm not saying not to dream. We'd better dream. The dream that Martin Luther King spoke of (and do not kid yourself, he too died in war), that dream is alive today. When I say that that his dream is alive, I do not mean that his dream is fully manifested. But I do mean that it was already done in the mind of God. I do know that this is the truth for Martin would not have been able to see it when he was in the earthly realm. He would not have been able to know it, were it not already done in the mind of God. This is consciousness I'm talking about. And consciousness has no past, no present and no future. Consciousness has no unforgiveness, no anger and no injustice. Consciousness is simply Love. Love has no boundaries. Love cannot be bound by a mortal coil. Love cannot be bound by a clock. Love cannot be contained in a holiday. Love

cannot be restricted by a war. Love cannot be expressed through any finite means.
The 109th psalm invites us to cut off the memory of them from the earth. Never mind the earthly realm. Fuggedaboutit! The 145th psalm tells us

> they shall abundantly utter the memory of thy great goodness,
> and shall sing of thy righteousness.

David is talking about the good of God, not the good of any man. He is talking about Spirit. Even Oprah talked about remembering spirit!
So maybe we need to stop talking about the way we were and step into the way we are. Perhaps we should step into our spiritual greatness. Perhaps we need to recognize our Beauty right now. Perhaps we need to recognize our capacity to Love is limitless. Perhaps we need to start now. Regardless of how it is framed in any language, words have no real meaning. Truth can be lived in silence. Indeed it is the only place that it does live. I am the I Am. Nothing can change it; no illusion of time or death can touch it. I am eternal. I am what I Am. Celebrate it - holiday or not! Embrace your divinity, your oneness with everything that is. Celebrate your eternal life and a Love that is everlasting.

DURING THIS PARTICULAR TIME

During this particular time
I chose <u>not</u> to call you.
This was not an option to entertain.
Yet you were there.

During this particular time,
I decided not to crawl into your big, strong, loving arms
and let you comfort me.
Yet you were there.

During this particular time,
I chose <u>not</u> to see your face.
You should not have allowed me to feel this empty.
Yet you were there.

During this particular time,
I had convinced myself that one of us
was not worthy of the other

and that I should not feel this despair.
Yet you were there.

During this particular time,
I chose not to think of you
for that would mean surrender.
Yet you were there.

During this particular time,
everywhere I turned, there was evidence of your presence.
I refuse to need you.
Yet you were there.

During this particular time,
you held me anyway.
I had no needs.
You were there.

WHEN THE WIND BLOWS

According to Matthew 14:28-32, Jesus, after having asked his disciples to get into a boat and go to the other side while he sent the multitudes away, dismissed the multitude and went up to the mountain to pray. Night came and the boat the disciples were in was being tossed by waves. Jesus went to them, walking on the sea. The disciples saw Jesus and cried out in fear. Jesus told them:

>It is I, be not afraid.

Peter told Jesus if it truly is him, to ask Peter to come to him. Jesus did. Peter was walking on the water. But when he saw that the wind was strong, he fell asking the Lord to save him. Jesus caught Peter and asked him why he doubted.
Jesus is from God. Jesus has skills. I have heard of many who perform miracles. Jesus must be one of them. But Jesus knew what Ernest Holmes later discovered:

>There is a power in the Universe that honors our faith in it.

One day a couple of years back, I heard a still small voice say, get up and move your car. I dismissed it. I thought at the time that I still had my mental chatter going on . I had not yet realized that I am in the circuit of God's flow. There's nothing outside of me. So, I went on doing those things that I thought I was supposed to do. When I went outside, there was no car where I was sure I had parked it. I called and found out that indeed they had towed my car just 15 minutes before I discovered its absence. I was not pleased. I had things to do. And I also happened to have had the exact amount of money required to get the car out of the private towing station it was in. $160. I had received $100 in the mail and a client had paid me $60 the day before. I had it. It was earmarked for something else. But I had it. I didn't even have to cry, Lord save me. He already had. He had saved me when he gave me the money. He was trying to save me when he said, come. Move the car. And I knew it sounded like my Master's voice. But I thought maybe it wasn't. Like Peter, I had been hanging out with my master long enough to know His voice.

The police towed my car away. But the Lord knew that I needed my car to do His work. God said you can do it on foot but it does not have to be that hard. Just listen to me. I received the thought more than once. God always tries to keep helping us.

Fillmore in his Metaphysical Bible Dictionary says that the walking on water story is a lesson in spiritual overcoming. Once that space within Peter knew the Christ was calling him, Peter commenced to walk on the water. And the water, fluid as it is, allowed Peter to walk on it. Peter was walking through his weakness into the field of potentiality. God is able to do all things. So here Peter is in the midst of all things possible.

Peter listened to his senses. He got scared. He's unstable. He falls. So now, instead of being in a sea of possibilities, he is in a sea of negativity. He's sinking into race consciousness. We do this sometimes when someone or something comes along that rains on our parade, throw us off *our* plans. We get afraid. We cry out, Lord, save me. And the Lord immediately does so. God loves us that much. He knows that instant.

Peter, who started out moving on the capacities of spirit consciousness when he's walking on water, began to sink in a sea of despair. Even those who have walked with Jesus could not see the reality. The Christ mind is our power that is ever available to us. When we have faith in it, everything is quieted. And I have faith that even in the harsh elements of my life, I am in harmony, wholeness and peace because it is my very thoughts that make it so. God makes it so through us as we are able to be still and know. Thank God for the Christ consciousness so that even when we lose our jobs, even when we lose the loves of our life, even when we lose parents, children, or when we lose our dreams, God is right there stretching out Its hand, catching us. God is holding us until we can know our own quiet, our own silence, our own calm, our own peace. So like Jesus, we can say to the wind, "Peace be still" because we are stillness. We are peace. By doing so, we are calling out to the All ness, the sea of possibilities for everything that we need for life.

A JOYFUL DIN

It's the end of the year
and we're full of cheer
And, of course, there's fear
when we're not being clear...

There's shopping
and bopping
And the Reverend is hopping
and fingers are popping...

and the faces
are smiling in places
cause people like joy
man, woman, girl and boy...

transgender too
and even the coy

release a laugh or a scream
as the faces beam

in the delight of Spirit and song
for the bliss is strong.

Meditation and prayer
without care
is the way we do church
when we're not in a lurch

to find parking
or tithe
cause the bodies will writhe

when the DJ spins
and the Spirit wins
over fear.

Then the Reindeer
are flying through space
with intent to erase
grown up despair
and go for a dare.

Dare to be free
to be up in the sky!
Dare to be now...
Dare to fly!

Not with alcohol or your drug of choice
but with God within – go ahead and rejoice

And declare to self and to all
It's holiday time – let's have a ball!

Come Ramadan, come Hanukkah,
Come Christmas and Kwanzaa

It's time to celebrate life
and release all the strife
of shopping and hopes of what might have been
thoughts of lost loved ones and packages to send

and embrace the joy of the season
remembering first and foremost the reason...

to be in Christ consciousness and know there's One
who will always love you and who's always fun

laughing with you, loving you, blessing you now
and bringing up stuff for you...showing you how

to embrace your freedom and let loose your joy
getting downright boisterous without being coy

but standing in your greatness and shining your light
releasing depression, anger and fright.

Knowing no separation by miles or by death
but embracing every new breath...

So dance in the harmony, the love and the peace
knowing the One Life will never cease.

Surrendering to the courage within
gives birth to a new life to begin
with goodwill toward men and wimmin

AND RAISING THE ROOF WITH A JOYFUL DIN!

So party on, party on, shake your groove thing.
It's time to give praises and love Self within!

WINTER OF DISCONTENT

There's something very cold about the winter of life. It feels lonely and the rays of the sun don't feel as warm in the last months of the year. It feels like a time to withdraw and seek to maintain our own inner warmth. We try to insulate ourselves from anything that might bring us discomfort. Yet underneath it all, even as the soil is being moistened, it is storing up all of the nutrients necessary for our rebirth in the Spring.

That's the Love Intelligence of God at work. While we are distracted by the external atmosphere, God is all the while preparing the space for us. Just as we are mourning the loss of summer or mourning the loss of someone outside of ourselves – our would-be savior, we are being saved for our new expansion. Even as we are looking to a messianic figure outside of us to rescue us, God is building up our inner strength.

How grateful I am to know God's Omniscience and Unconditional Love. Were I responsible for figuring it all out, I would be stuck in the minutia of the material details. Even then, I would be taken care of; but who knows when I would wake up to realize it! I'm grateful that God knows and holds my good as It waits patiently for me to awaken to It. Better than a federally insured bank account, more stable than a CD with interest, God holds my interest and is interested in my good.

As a child of God, I can infinitely receive my birthright. I need only be vigilant to the reading of God's will. In the stillness, I listen.

WRITING

Writing is powerful because it makes me stop. Once I've stopped, writing becomes a reality check. I mean a real Reality check. I am in touch with the Presence and Its Creativity. I am in touch with my creative self. It's not something I recognize and yet it is something that I want to take credit for doing -- most of the time. That most of the time is qualified as that time when I am really writing. That time when I am just tapped into the Source and I'm not even there. The "I" is that I that identifies with external things in the world, earthly things, physical things, material things, temporary things. Writing that is an assignment, a duty, a responsibility or a task is not real writing. That I've done. And I've done that with rewriting. I've diluted my own writing to please others. I've diluted my writing in order to fit into someone s idea of what it was supposed to look like. Writing outside of the Self is not writing. The only true writing is that which comes from the heart. The heart space is the point where Spirit is clear and unbounded. It is the space where the Presence is having its way with me.

BIBLIOGRAPHY

Bannerji, Debashish. <u>Upanishads And the Bhagavad Gita</u>. Los Angeles: Philosophical Research Society, 1998.

Braden, Charles S. <u>Spirits in Rebellion, The Rise and Development of New Thought</u>. Dallas, TX: Southern Methodist University Press, 1987.

Butterworth, Eric. <u>Spiritual Economics</u>, Unity Village, MO: Unity House, 2001.

Corbett, Lionel, M.D. <u>A New Myth of God</u>. Los Angeles: Philosophical Research Society, 1997.

Dass, Ram, <u>How Can I Help</u>. New York and Toronto, Canada: Alfred A. Knopf, Inc., 1985.

Dreamer, Oriah Mountain. <u>The Invitation</u>. San Francisco: Harper Collins Publishers, 1999.

Filmore, Charles. <u>Metaphysical Bible Dictionary</u>. Unity Village, MO: Unity Books, 1931.

Goldsmith, Joel S. <u>Practicing the Presence</u>. San Francisco: Harper Collins Publishers, 1958.

Holmes, Ernest. <u>The Science of Mind</u>. New York: Penguin Putnam Inc., 1998.

<u>The Holy Bible, The Open Bible Edition</u>. Nashville, TN: Thomas Nelson Inc., 1975.

Lamsa, George M. <u>Holy Bible, From the Ancient Eastern Text</u>. New York: A.J. Holman Co., 1939.

Lamsa, George M. <u>Old Testament Light</u>. New York: Harper & Row Publishers, 1964.

Levine, Ondrea, and Levine, Stephen. <u>Embracing the Beloved</u>. New York: Anchor Books, 1996.

Merriam-Webster. <u>Webster's College Dictionary</u>. New York: Random House, 1991.

Palmer, Parker J. <u>To Know As We Are Known</u>. San Francisco: Harper Collins Publishers, 1993.

Werber, Eva Bell, <u>The Journey With the Master</u>. Camarillo, CA: DeVorss & Company, 1950.

Made in the USA
Coppell, TX
10 January 2022

71405471R00066